THE BUILDING CONSERVATION DIRECTORY
SPECIAL REPORT ON HISTORIC GARDEN LANDSCAPES

Special Report N° 2, First Edition

November 1994

ISBN 0 9520080 4 1

PUBLISHED BY
Cathedral Communications Limited
66 Strathleven Road,
London, England SW2 5LB
0171 738 6462

MANAGING DIRECTOR
Gordon Sorensen

EXECUTIVE EDITOR
Jonathan Taylor

HORTICULTURE EDITOR
Philip Swindells

MARKETING, PROMOTIONS DIRECTOR
Elizabeth Coyle-Camp

ADVERTISING SALES
Michael Porter

RESEARCH
Lisa Oestreicher
Janis Leith

PRODUCTION
Xendo, London

PRINTING
Optichrome, Woking

FRONT COVER ILLUSTRATION

Sundial in Rose Pergola, **Newby Hall and Gardens**, Ripon, North Yorkshire, by kind permission of R.E.J. Compton Esq. (Hall and Gardens open April–September)

contents

A WORD FROM THE EDITOR

Never before has there been such a great interest in our gardening heritage. Visitor numbers are increasing each year and extraordinary pressures are now being placed upon some of our finest historic gardens and landscapes. These pressures are both physical and financial and are a new experience for most garden managers and owners. This Special Report looks at many of the issues which affect historic gardens today and seeks to serve as a useful reference which will help take our garden heritage safely into the next century.

Philip Swindells

Philip Swindells studied horticulture at the University of Cambridge Botanic Gardens. He has over 30 years experience managing and advising upon historic and botanical gardens.

THE NEED FOR PROTECTION

DAVID LAMBERT
Conservation Officer
Garden History
Society

WHILE the value of parks and gardens has been recognised by visitors and owners for centuries, official recognition of their importance as part of the national heritage and environment has come only very recently. Although the 1974 Town and Country Amenities Act had extended Listed Building legislation to the settings of buildings and had also identified designed landscapes as worthy in their own right of grant-aid, no new funds were actually made available and so the first effective recognition only came in the 1983 National Heritage Act. This empowered the newly formed English Heritage to prepare a register of gardens, parks and designed landscapes of special historic interest. The register is thus a statutory document, although it is advisory only and sites included are subject to no additional statutory controls.

In the remarkably short period 1984-88 English Heritage completed its Register of parks and gardens of special historic interest, which comprised a set of county volumes containing outline histories and site descriptions of just over a thousand sites. As a result of subsequent additions and the revision currently underway, the number of registered sites now stands at 1,213, and the written descriptions have been augmented with boundary maps.

The decision on whether or not a site merits inclusion on the Register is the responsibility of English Heritage's Inspector of Parks and Gardens, who at present is Dr Harriet Jordan. The Inspector is advised and supported as necessary by the Head of Listing and by English Heritage's Historic Parks and Gardens Committee, on which a number of external experts sit. The historic interest is judged in a national context and the Register is thus a fairly exclusive list of sites of national importance. By way of comparison, in the county of Avon's gazetteer of 289 sites of local importance only 20 were included on the original volume of the Register (another 10 have been added subsequently).

The nature, size and age of sites included varies enormously and commendably. As well as 18th Century landscape parks and 19th Century gardens there are earthwork remains such as Chipping Campden and Holdenby; areas of planned urban development such as London squares or the Backs at Cambridge; walks such as the New Walk in Leicester and Beckford's Ride outside Bath; cemeteries; Edwardian and Victorian public parks; plantsman's gardens with valuable collections. The chronological span is comprehensive, the latest site being Harlow New Town Water Gardens and the earliest being a number of mediaeval deer parks, while sizes vary from one to a thousand hectares.

The Register has been invaluable in affording for the first time official recognition of the importance of parks and gardens as part of the heritage and environment. Its existence facilitated the introduction of grant-aid for repairs, kick-started by the hurricanes of 1987 and 1990, and it also brought parks and gardens into the planning system on a semi-formal basis: 'semi-formal' because of the anomalous status of a statutory but merely advisory list.

Warwick Castle: View from Guys Tower.

The role of the Register in the planning system varies depending on county and local authorities. The only national framework was afforded by DoE Circular 8/87 now superseded by the new Planning Policy Guidance Note 15. The Circular stressed the desirability of safeguarding registered sites and most county authorities responded with a general policy on historic parks and gardens in the structure plan. The extent to which in turn local authorities then introduced a policy in the local plan is much more erratic.

The weight given to the importance of parks and gardens in planning decisions again varies enormously, at all levels including the Planning Inspectorate. There is little doubt that this still depends greatly on the individual case made either by owners, amenity societies, historians, conservation officers or English Heritage.

Despite the very sketchy national guidance on parks and gardens, at a local and county level there are many initiatives which are being or can be taken. Policies in development plans apart, these initiatives include the designation of Conservation Areas, either including or wholly comprising a historic landscape; the use of Article 4 directions to restrict permitted development; the inclusion of parks and gardens on the County Council's Sites and Monuments Record, which brings them under the umbrella protecting archaeological sites; the preparation of supplementary planning guidance or strategies on parks and gardens; the use of Tree Preservation Orders; and the introduction of grant-aid for restoration or enhancement projects. Most parks and gardens are already covered by the statutory duty to protect the settings of listed buildings, whether a central house or individual garden structures.

In Wales, the National Heritage Act 1983, did not empower Cadw to produce a Register. They have, however, followed the English pattern and one county register has been published (Gwent) and another is ready for publication (Clwyd), while work is in progress on others. Because of the lack of a statutory basis for these Registers, it is possible for the owner of a site to refuse to allow it to be included, and this has occurred in a very few cases. In other ways, the situation in Wales is similar to that in England.

In Scotland the pattern has been rather different. There has been no primary legislation referring to parks and gardens. However, in 1987 a joint initiative by the Countryside Commission for Scotland (now part of Scottish Natural Heritage) and the Historic Buildings and Monuments Directorate of the Scottish Development Department (now Historic Scotland) led to the production of the Inventory of Gardens and Designed Landscapes. This was not intended to include all sites that met a certain standard, but rather a representative sample of the best sites and 275 were included. Urban parks and cemeteries were deliberately excluded (unless there was some other reason for their inclusion, such as the fact that the park was based on an earlier designed park). There is now a programme to extend the Inventory and up to 100 additional sites will be included. This time urban parks will not be excluded.

The Inventory is referred to in secondary legislation. The Town and Country Planning (General Development Procedures) (Scotland)

Warwick Castle: View from Spiers Lodge.

Order of 1992 requires all local authorities to consult both Historic Scotland and Scottish Natural Heritage over any proposal affecting a site on the Inventory. It is perhaps too early to assess the effectiveness of the mechanism.

Some local authorities, both regional (e.g. Grampian) and district (Gordon) councils, have also produced their own lists of parks and gardens of historic interest and planning policies to protect them.

THE WAY FORWARD

Whether or not further measures, to introduce a statutory duty on owners and local authorities to conserve registered sites, are necessary or desirable is a moot point. English Heritage thinks not; many pressure groups and planning officers disagree.

On the one hand, the anomalous and unpredictable status of parks and gardens in the planning system is hardly satisfactory. Not only pressure groups but planners are complaining about it. In the wake of the Warwick Castle park public inquiry, when a hotel and golf-club scheme was rejected by the Secretary of State, a call for statutory definition of the status of historic landscapes even came from a firm of planning consultants on behalf of owners and prospective developers. Parks and gardens are an important part of the heritage – landscape gardening has been called the country's greatest contribution to European culture – and their importance is recognised in terms of grants of public money. For other elements in the heritage which receive grant-aid, some form of control is accepted as a natural corollary.

On the other hand, English Heritage and many owners point out the inherent difficulty of 'controlling' a park or garden; something in which, unlike buildings or ancient monuments, change is fundamental. The Government too is generally opposed on ideological grounds to what it sees as interference with private property rights.

In a discussion paper on statutory protection last year, the Garden History Society proposed a distinction between the structural and decorative elements in a landscape. This suggested that the structure – which has, whether in the siting of features, the lines of hedges or the configuration of tree-planting, an element of permanence – could be defined and protected, while the decoration – such as the flower-planting, which not only requires continuous change but which also has least long-term impact on the historic character of a place – could be left free of controls and the much-dreaded bureaucratic interference. The paper suggested that the structure of historic parks and gardens needed protection from major, irreversible harm. Despite its clumsiness and the evident examples where – a Jekyll border for example – the historic interest might reside in the decoration, the distinction has met with a good deal of approval, even while the principle remains contentious.

Statutory control could take many forms. At its simplest it could be the introduction of a duty on owners and local authorities to have regard to the desirability of (in Conservation Area terminology) preserving or enhancing the character or appearance of registered gardens without any specific new procedures. A more elaborate version would be the introduction of some kind of Registered Garden Consent, whereby works which materially affected the character or appearance of a site would require planning permission. This would have the advantage of bringing under control those types of development which do harm parks and gardens, but which at present do not require planning permission – such as the construction of swimming pools in gardens or of new agricultural buildings or access roads in parks.

As for the future, much can be done in terms of education. The hostility of many owners towards 'bureaucrats', usually meaning planners and conservationists, is hardly a tribute to the role of experts in areas where controls already exist, whether listed buildings, conservation areas, ancient monuments or sites of special scientific interest – all of which were considered by the GHS paper in terms of the models they afforded. 'Advice' all too often comes over as meddling and obstruction, and the dearth of expertise on historic parks and gardens is certainly a problem in considering any new controls.

English Heritage's resources are over-stretched and cannot deal with the existing flow of requests for advice on registered gardens. Expertise at local and county levels is even thinner; only two counties and no local authorities have historic landscape officers. There is plainly a time lag behind the introduction of the Register into the planning system and the education of decision-makers. But the academic world is responding: training courses and events on garden history and garden conservation are becoming much more common, and lack of expertise must be a short-term problem.

The GHS and English Heritage have also proposed to Government the introduction of a requirement on local authorities to consult formally on planning applications which affect registered sites. At present, such consultation is voluntary and patchy, and so harmful development can get through or at least proceed far down the planning process without any expert comment. English Heritage and the GHS learn of planning applications at present on an ad hoc basis and a formal procedure would at the very least allow us to monitor what is happening to registered sites. The Government has replied that it is 'sympathetic' to the introduction of such a requirement.

Historic parks and gardens are new arrivals in official consciousness with a status which is uncertain and ill-defined. Parkland in particular, comprising as it does large areas of open land often adjacent to urban centres or to major roads, is highly vulnerable to development pressure of all kinds. Over the next few years, that uncertainty must be resolved if we are not to see many more sites succumb to that pressure. ✳

HISTORIC AUTHENTICITY
How Far Should You Go?

PHILIP SWINDELLS
Special Report
Horticulture Editor
looks at the some of the
practical difficulties in
choosing the 'right'
flowering plant varieties

Rosa Mundi (Rosa gallica 'Versicolor'): a genuine
old rose but superceded by modern varieties of
old fashioned appearance

Bellis perennis 'Robella': a modern long flowering and
trouble free version of the old invasive cushion daisy

ONE of the greatest quandaries for the owner or manager of an historic garden or landscape is the necessity for the re-establishment of authentic plant material. Should well researched garden history restrict a garden to the plants that were there before, or should a progressive but sympathetic stance be taken?

Putting aside the question of the correctness of attempting to freeze a garden in a fixed period and the practical difficulties of doing so, there is always going to be a conflict between the researcher in his quest for authenticity, and the gardener or manager who has to cope with the current day constraints of garden management including the need for visitor enjoyment where the garden is open to the public.

Before considering the very real practical management problems that using genuine historic plants can create there are more important ones of provenance. With most plants that were introduced before the turn of the century there is considerable variability. Sometimes this is the natural variation of species which occurs in the wild, but equally, open pollinated cultivars can exhibit considerable genetic variation. Even vegetatively propagated plants from an earlier period can show differences in habit and behaviour because propagules were taken from varied stock.

In the general context of restored planting this does not create a problem, for it is quite clear that if a strain of seed-raised flowers was used to produce the effect of a garden in the Elizabethan period, wide variation would be exhibited in the plants. This can be achieved by using stock from varying sources, but today these would not necessarily be of even remotely similar provenance to that used in the period, even though it may look outwardly the same.

Nowadays much of the flower seed that we buy in Europe is grown on contract for seed companies in south east Asia or South America. It will have undergone modern tests for germination or purity, but its origins will be lost in the mists of time. Indeed, if of a species of cosmopolitan distribution it may well contain mixed populations of seed from different continents. The mixing and blending of seeds has taken place for decades and creates broad genetic bases which are impossible to disentangle.

It is also important to realise that over the years man has slowly changed the plants which he is growing by selection. Often unwittingly by choosing the strongest growing or brightest coloured plants as seed bearers he has through several generations altered their characteristics considerably. A recent example of this can be demonstrated by the experience of a Scandinavian botanical garden which grows a selection of annual plants to demonstrate the diversity of the plant kingdom to botany students. These plants were always grown in natural order beds, family by family, and each year the gardener gathered his own seed and sowed it again the following year. For 150 years this continued with no apparent differences in appearance of the plants. Subconsciously the gardener responsible always gathered seeds from the finest looking plants.

The botanical garden recently changed its policy to only growing plants of known wild provenance. Plants that would have a field reference, would exhibit typical characteristics of the natural population and if necessary could be used as sources of **ex situ** conservation material. To the surprise of everybody some of the species which had

The reintroduction of wild collected plants like these irises may bring genuine authenticity, but major cultural problems.

proved to be perfectly satisfactory in cultivation previously no longer responded in the same way. Growth was patchy and unsatisfactory. What had clearly occurred in the past was the creation of a selection which over the years had produced the kind of population which the gardener and teacher required, but which no longer bore much resemblance to the plants of the same species which were being grown in that botanical garden 150 years earlier. The plant had moved on with the passage of time and the reintroduction of wild gathered material, which in all probability was similar to that grown 150 years ago, would not now satisfy the other requirements of the garden, except for those of the pure academic.

An historic garden which is open to the public will have considerable difficulty in

explaining the inconsistency of growth displayed by the genuine article when the visitor is paying for a different kind of experience. Even if it were sensible to present plantings in this way, there is no guarantee that the wild population itself would have not changed in some way from that of 150 years ago. So even when precise collection data is available, genuine authentic restoration is difficult to guarantee. If this is the case, then surely it is sensible to take a broad view and if a particular species is deemed to be historically correct for the garden feature, then let us not be too concerned about its origin and if it has been visually and culturally improved we should be able to live with it.

This then moves towards another controversial area. If modern selections of historic plant species and open pollinated cultivars can be condoned, is there a case where cultural difficulties occur of using closely allied forms or cultivars which provide the same, or a similar visual effect? The use of some of the modern shrub rose cultivars, which are indistinguishable to the garden visiting public from the old fashioned kinds, would seem to confer benefits of greater disease resistance and often perpetual flowering upon a rose garden, which in all but academic authenticity could be the same as existed at that period of the garden. Decisions of this nature must be based upon the role the garden plays. Is it a strictly authentic educational and conservation feature, or must it derive its income from satisfied visitors?

There is an alternative argument which can be posed under these circumstances and that is one of plant conservation. It is assumed that our historic gardens and landscapes are the repository for many of our disappearing garden plants. To a great extent this is true, although in many cases the holdings of our historic gardens are not documented. This is a task which needs addressing, but until statutory bodies take as much interest in our garden plant heritage as they do in inanimate artefacts, then much of what our historic gardens and landscapes maintain will remain unknown.

The National Council for the Conservation of Plants and Gardens has made a brave start in learning of what remains of the plants of the past, the most innovative initiative being to establish National Plant Collections. These are subjected to strict but sensible rules and are being established genus by genus and

distributed throughout the country. Ideally there is not a single national collection, but two or three which can provide an insurance against pests and disease decimation and also give gardeners an opportunity to see the same cultivars performing under different conditions in various parts of the country. This provides valuable information about the behaviour of individual cultivars.

Many of our best historic gardens contain collections of old cultivars. Often they have become designated national collections, but many are just important assemblages of allied plants that are no longer available in commerce. This stewardship is absolutely vital, for although in the recreation of the art and history of a garden the use of alternatives to the original species or cultivar can often be justified, the loss of the genetic base of our heritage plants is unforgivable. On both scientific and historical grounds it is essential that we care for our past, but reusing the plants in the same manner is not always appropriate in those cases where both conservation and visitor enjoyment are important.

We must never lose sight of the fact that if we wish to retain our garden heritage and conserve the historically important plants of the past, we must find the means to finance it. In some cases there are philanthropic garden owners who maintain their collections from other sources than the garden. This is fine if it is sustainable. Establishing a garden in such a way that visitors fund it, although not ideal, is usually the most sustainable method of providing finance and sharing our garden heritage with others. In these cases the issue of the conservation of garden plants needs to be addressed separately.

In some cases plants which are important historically can be accommodated within the general planting of the garden without impediment. However, from the point of view of a collection it is often easier to manage and more appealing when the plants are grown in close proximity. The fact that some will only perform tolerably well compared with their modern counterparts is of little concern, for in this context the plants are part of a collection and to some extent reflect the history of that plant group. Indeed, the plant collection assembled in this manner, apart from being of conservation merit, can by careful interpretation become an added feature to the garden which is of great interest to visitors. ✄

Philip Swindells is the principal of Philip Swindells Associates, international horticultural consultants specialising in the management, restoration and conservation of historic parks and gardens.
Both a Nuffield and Mary Helliar Scholar he has a wide experience of garden management both at home and overseas and is the author of twenty six books on horticultural topics.

INVESTIGATING HISTORIC GARDEN AND LANDSCAPE DESIGN

DR. J. A. ROBERTS

Blickling Hall, Aylsham, Norfolk where architecture and structural planting mass together. The moat has been dry since the early 17th Century.

All photos provided by the author.

HISTORIC parks and gardens are a rich and important part of our cultural heritage. Since the formation of the Garden History Society in 1965 and the publication of the first editions of the *'Register of Historic Parks and Gardens of Special Historic Interest in England'* by English Heritage in the 1980s there has been a growing public awareness of the value of parks and gardens, not only as cultural objects in their own right but also for the contribution they make to the character and texture of the rural and urban environment. An increasing number of local authorities are now including policies for the protection of parks and gardens in their local plans and undertaking stock taking exercises to raise awareness and to establish the nature of local characteristics. Grant aid for restoration or conservation does exist

under schemes like the newly established English Heritage gardens grants schemes or the Historic Landscapes Option of the Countryside Commission's wider Countryside Stewardship Scheme but funds are always limited and modest and the grant depends, to some extent, on the outcome of historical survey work. It is always important for the understanding and the future of the site that the historical survey should be done thoroughly and well. The contribution of the historian is vital since it is the skills of the historian which will establish the history of the site and set it in its context.

It is important to establish a framework for historical research since much of the work undertaken in connection with historic parks and gardens will have a practical outcome and will be the springboard for the decision making

process. Research will, for example, be the basis on which planning or management decisions will be made, it will influence the outcome of funding and grant applications and the setting of priorities in the allocation of resources and money. Indeed, research into the history and development of a site is a vital component in its effective management and conservation and a soundly researched analysis of its historical profile is the only secure basis on which any site can be carried forward into the future.

First of all it is worth thinking about what makes an historic park or garden; what is the constellation of characteristics or attributes which combine together to create a site which has local or national historic significance?

Plants, and particularly structural planting, are important and sometimes, in a plantsman's garden, plants are the most important feature. However, historic gardens are much more than collections of plant material and in many cases the horticultural interest may be limited or less significant than other characteristics or design associations. There are exceptions but architecture is nearly always an important element and many historic gardens have an architectural structure, a house or even a bandstand or fountain, as the focus of their composition. Indeed, changes in the function and furnishing of rooms in a house or in shifting patterns of

part of our wider cultural and physical landscape. They are the repositories of past ideas and preoccupations through which we can touch and interpret the aspirations of their creators. In the grouping and massing of buildings, structural planting and the orchestration of architectural and spatial elements we can read the development of design and taste and it this chronological layering which is often one of the most important distinguishing characteristics of a site of historic significance. Historic parks and gardens frequently also have a complement of designed views, in and out, which knit the site and its context together and through which they enter the wider cultural and physical landscape.

An historic park or garden is a complex structure and a full programme of research will be an inter-disciplinary activity which will depend on the co-ordination and co-operation of a team of professional experts. Investigating, and explaining the development of the site over time is the historian's particular contribution and will depend on the interpretation of a range of documents and materials. What are these materials and how can they be used?

Every site is different but there are a number of common approaches and archive research is usually one of the starting points. The creation of an 18th Century ornamental landscape or a 19th Century municipal park was a major undertaking requiring the production of plans, maps and drawings, written directions and financial accounts. It is through such documents that we can observe the process of construction and it is also through them that we can allow contemporaries to speak to us. Indeed, it is only by establishing this contemporary perspective that we can interpret, and effectively conserve, what we see today.

Large-scale garden designs and landscaping schemes were always expensive and Humphry Repton's 'Red Books' are an

excellent and well known example of an effective sales technique but council minutes are just as illuminating, if less spectacularly presented, in understanding the creation, the gradual accumulation of land and the discussions and arguments surrounding the design decisions of urban parks. Sets of dated plans and drawings and the large scale Ordnance Survey maps studied together illustrate the development of a site over time in response to an owner's whim or the changes of fashion, and diaries and journals record the details and the response of contemporaries to such changes.

Plans, drawings and account books are vital source material for particular sites and they can also be marvellously supplemented by the wealth of contemporary printed texts and illustrations which became increasingly common from the late 16th Century onwards. County histories and later the Victoria County History describe particular properties and set them within their local context. Engravings like those published by Knyff and Kip as *'Britannia Illustrata'* during the first half of the 18th Century illustrate 'bird's eye' views of country estates. These views may sometimes be exaggerated but a careful analysis leads to an understanding of the intended relationship between various parts of the design and the interconnection of the garden and pleasure ground with its agricultural estate and the wider landscape setting.

The 19th Century brought an explosion of published gardening literature linked, to a great extent, with the rapid development of the town and the suburban villa. Many of these texts were aimed at the newly rich and carry a great emphasis on 'taste'. Shirley Hibberd's works are an example of this genre and contain a wealth of illustrative and descriptive detail which raise awareness of the design intentions of the gardens and entrances of the urban villa residence and also aid the recognition of the value of summer houses and rustic seats and shelters, the remnants of Victorian middle class

Burton Agnes Hall, Humberside. Built by Robert Smythson in 1598–1610. Moving water has always been an important feature in gardens and fountains and cascades continue to be added to the overlays of an historic site.

public use and behaviour around structures in an urban park will often be reflected in the changes in the garden or landscape design; architectural and landscape development should always be researched together. Historic gardens can also be seen as galleries for the display of rich cultural objects like statues, urns and decorative vases which may have distinct and discrete interest in their own right as well as collective importance as part of an overall design composition. Fountains, cascades and moving water have a long history as design elements in sites like Chatsworth, Castle Howard and a host of public parks. These places are gardens and pleasure grounds but they are no less engineering sites whose functioning, maintenance and conservation depend on a sound knowledge of hydraulics.

Finally, historic parks and gardens are

Part of a plan showing the layout of Bore Place near Chiddingstone in Kent, 1765.
There is a small garden divided into squares with a statue at the intersection of the walks. This is divided from a second garden and flanked by water features, possibly fish ponds. The plan shows the close connection between the house, garden and the agricultural estate.[Reproduced by kind permission of the Centre for Kentish Studies, Maidstone]

Top left and right. Rydal Hall, Cumbria. The formal garden laid out by Thomas Mawson c1909 uses structures and views to link the site with the surrounding countryside but this is only one layer in its history. Slightly beyond these gardens is a small building replacing a 'grotto' of similar design which has stood in this position from at least the late 17th Century to enjoy the view of what William Gilpin described as 'a considerable stream, falling down a quick descent, along a rocky channel'.
Bottom left. Architecture and planting overcome the flatness of the landscape at Shugborough. The Chinese House is also an historical record in its own right recalling Admiral Anson's visit to Canton in 1743.
Bottom right. Burton Agnes Hall, Humberside. Sun dial and garden furniture – a reminder of what a garden is for!

aspirations. Finally there is the impact of photography and the rise of popular journals and magazines. Country Life is one of the best and its superb photographs contain a wealth of material to illustrate the details of planting and layout of the sites it describes.

These are examples of some of the main groups of source material available for researching the history and contemporary context of a site. Allied to this, and in some cases the absolute test of an interpretation, is archaeological site investigation. Excavation will actually destroy evidence but where reconstruction is the aim, as for example at the Privy Garden, Hampton Court, digging, and scrupulous recording is the only way to establish the exact details of layout, shape, size and the nuances of development and adaptation. Behind all this is the best document of all, the site itself. Careful reading of its elements and the layers of its development which they reveal is a necessary adjunct to documentary research. Indeed, documents cannot be used in isolation but must be interpreted together with a reading and understanding of the physical features of the site.

This is an introduction to some of the methods of investigation which have been developed to serve the investigation of larger, long established sites, but now there is a challenge. There is much more to our park and garden heritage than 18th Century country estates and 19th Century municipal parks. As popular interest grows and widens there is increasing awareness of vernacular gardens and of the design, survival and local characteristics of cottage, villa or even suburban gardens. Researching these gardens will require the development of new approaches, the refinement of research methods and perhaps a reinvestigation of what we mean by 'historic'. Gardens are, of course, alive and dynamic, they develop and change and it is fitting that our approach to their research and understanding should also be open to change. Indeed, it is the excitement of change and development which makes this particular area of historical research so rewarding. ▓

FURTHER READING
Journals
❖ Garden History. The Journal of the Garden History Society
❖ Journal of Garden History. An International Quarterly editor John Dixon Hunt, London and Washington DC

Printed Works
❖ Mavis Batey and David Lambert *The English Garden Tour A View Into The Past,* John Murray, London 1990
❖ Hazel Conway and David Lambert *Public Prospects Historic Parks Under Threat* A Garden History Society and Victorian Society Report, London 1994
❖ Miles Hadfield *A History of British Gardening* Penguin Books 1985
❖ John Harvey *Restoring Period Gardens* Shire Publications 1988
❖ David Lambert *Researching a Garden's History* Centre for the Conservation of Historic Parks and Gardens, IOAAS, University of York, 1991

Dr. Judith Roberts is a Research Fellow at the Institute of Advanced Architectural Studies, the University of York where she runs the Historic Parks and Gardens Research Unit specialising in survey work and the study of vernacular gardens. She has lectured on subjects related to the history and conservation of parks and gardens in this country and in China and is currently working on a number of publications concerned with vernacular gardens and survey methodology.

The **IOAAS** runs a number of short courses dealing with all aspects of the conservation of historic parks and gardens. A Gardens and Landscape Option may be taken as part of the MA in Conservation Studies.
For further information on all conservation courses telephone 01904 433982, fax 01904 433949

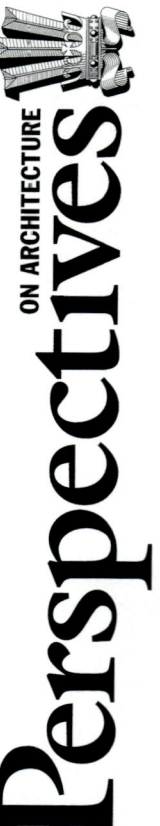

The restored conservatory at Whittlingham near Norwich.

IRON-FRAMED CONSERVATORIES AND GREENHOUSES

Despite the tragic destruction of many delightful examples over the years, iron conservatories are relatively simple to repair.

BRIAN MORTON

THE structure and construction of conservatories is a fascinating subject. The advent of the Industrial Revolution was the prime factor in their development. As people's wealth improved it became quite a status symbol to have a conservatory for propagating plants, and considerable progress was made over a comparatively short period in their design.

Although buildings were constructed as a form of conservatory as early as the end of the 16th Century, these structures, known as 'orangeries', were masonry structures incorporating a substantial amount of glass. It was not until the invention in 1816 by John Claudius Loudon of a wrought iron sash bar that could be bent in any direction without reducing its strength that the development of conservatories and greenhouses took a step forward. Using these glazing bars to form curves, he developed the "Ridge & Furrow" curvilinear glass houses that were the predecessors of Chatsworth (1838–1840) and the Crystal Palace (1850–1851) both by Joseph Paxton, a stalwart in the development of iron structures. From 1815 to the end of the 19th Century with the development of new furnaces to make cast iron on a large scale, greenhouses and conservatories rapidly developed into new forms using cast iron frameworks with glazed frames between. These kits of parts were easily fabricated and became very popular.

Corrosion that caused the investigation at **Whittlingham Hospital, Norwich**, dealt with by taking the frame apart, derusting and repainting.

The glazing bar in the roof of the conservatory at **Whittlingham Hospital, Norwich** showing the corrosion bursting of the lead covering to the glazing bar.

The earlier curvilinear buildings, simply by their form of design, stand up extremely well if they are maintained to a reasonable level. However, their integrity relies on the interlinking of all their structural elements. Failure of one glazing bar imposes additional load on the next, thus there can be an escalating effect if repairs are not made to the failed members. Generally in all these conservatories the screws holding the sections together can be simply unscrewed and it is possible to take out the individual sections of bars that have deteriorated and replace them with new wrought iron or steel.

There are many misunderstandings about the reasons for the deterioration of these conservatories; generally the only cause is corrosion. The form of construction is always a main frame which generally has rebated principal posts and the window frames simply fit into them. Usually it is found that there is a gap around the windows into the rebate of the main post and as a result it is a long time before corrosion really takes a hold, with real problems occurring in structures about a hundred years after the initial construction. Maintenance is therefore vital, particularly for older structures. The first signs of red rust should be investigated and the source of the water that is causing the corrosion dealt with before the situation gets beyond control.

My early involvement in conservatory repair started with a request from The Victorian Society to look at the conservatory at Old Catton, near Norwich because it was suggested that it was going to cost £250,000 to restore. I realised it was simply a kit of parts and after some investigation we found it quite possible to take the conservatory apart. We successfully specified the repair techniques and were able to complete the restoration of the building for approximately £45,000.

This commission led on to our involvement in restoring the Conservatory at Whittlingham Hospital, near Norwich. The problem there was very similar to Old Catton although the form of construction was somewhat different and it was suggested by other professionals involved that there was foundation movement. On further investigation we realised that the problems were simply caused by the development of rust between the various components and in essence all that was required was to take sections of the conservatory apart, repair them and fix them back together. In this case, however the glazing bars were a form of wrought iron covered in lead, which had been made by an extrusion process. They had worked quite satisfactorily for a life of about eighty years, but corrosion was taking over and the lead was bursting away from the glazing bars. We considered using stainless steel or aluminium, but were fortunate to find the original manufacturer of the glazing bars still used the same process and we were able to obtain replacements.

An important factor in the repair and restoration process is the careful sand-blasting of all elements of the structure and the painting of the iron with a suitable specification such as two coats of zinc-rich paint with a chlorinated rubber finishing paint. Reglazing should incorporate as much of the early glass as can be removed without breakage, as early glass has an appearance and historic interest which is quite unique. We have carried out reglazing using silicone mastic in accordance with the recommendations of the specialist glazing firms involved in this work.

These iron conservatories need to be understood and as part of the initial investigation some opening up is necessary. Following a recent call to look at Broughton Hall Conservatory, near Liverpool it was suggested the conservatory should be demolished because of structural movement. I found very little wrong with the basic structure but felt that some investigation was necessary. The cast iron building was a very unusual construction with glass set between

The restored conservatory at **Old Catton near Norwich**, where original estimates suggested it was going to cost £250,000 to restore and it was actually restored for £45,000.

The elevation of the un-restored conservatory at **Glevering Hall in Suffolk**.

The bursting of the column at **Glevering Hall in Suffolk** brought about by the corrosion of cast iron dowl bars and the corrosion of horizontal ties.

the glazed frieze which ran all the way round the conservatory. This led me to wonder how it had been put together. Investigations showed that there was a light timber frame placed between two halves of the cast iron circular columns. In the event, it was not a particular problem but it was absolutely vital that we knew of the form of construction before preparing our specification.

Orangeries have their own particular sources of problems. At Glevering Hall in Suffolk the main structure consisted of stone pillars supporting a timber and cast iron roof. The roof itself is in quite excellent condition for its age, but unfortunately the stonework of the pillars had been erected with iron clamps between the stones in the columns and horizontal ties across the large windows had been built into the stonework. The iron has rusted and

is bursting the stonework at probably 50 per cent of the joints. Analysis of the structure showed that the roof could be temporarily supported, the vertical windows taken out and the stone disassembled, the iron clamps removed and the whole put back together again. Discussions with contractors suggested that this was much the cheapest and easiest way of dealing with this problem.

To sum up, the repair of iron conservatories is generally not difficult and demolition should not be considered. Although it is generally not understood, the repair of these structures is a comparatively inexpensive operation because where a section of decorated ironwork needs to be replaced, a mould can easily be made up from that section and a new section cast. With the advent of firms now manufacturing wrought iron, new sections of glazing bar can be manufactured and welded to the old. The general rule is to make sure that waterways that were built into the original design are kept clear and the structure is kept painted using a proper metal paint specification. ▨

RECOMMENDED READING

❖ John Gloag *Mr Louden's England* Oriel Press, 1970
❖ Georg Kohlmaier and Barna von Sartory *Houses of Glass* MIT Press 1981 *(This is really the Bible for the serious reader)*.
❖ May Woods and Arete Warren *Glass and Houses* Aurum Press 1988
❖ Various authors *The English Garden Room* Weindenfeld & Nicholson, London 1986
❖ Ann Bonar *The Conservatory Handbook*
❖ *Structural Aspects of Croom* Helm Publishers 1986
❖ Alan Toogood *The Conservatory for Plants and People* Ward Lock, London 1985

Brian Morton now acts as Consultant to The Morton Partnership Ltd., a firm that he originally formed in 1966.

He is currently the Engineer to Lincoln Cathedral and for the restoration of the Albert Memorial and the Fire of London Monument in London.

He has been involved in the restoration of conservatories over the last ten years and spends his time advising clients of the most cost effective and minimum interference schemes for the restoration of historic structures.

Garden Statuary

Fine statuary forms a key element in the garden landscape but it is vulnerable to decay, demanding sensitive care and conservation.

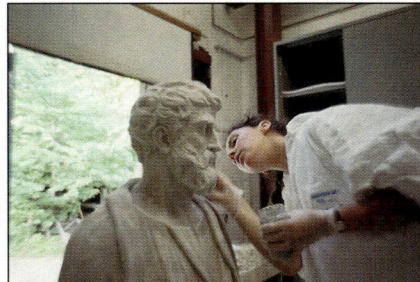

Casting of a replica Scheemaker sculpture of an ancient worthy for the temple of Ancient Virtue, Stowe, Buckinghamshire.

All photos provided by the author.

TREVOR PROUDFOOT

IT is an unavoidable fact that all statuary and monuments decay from the moment they are made, and the garden environment is, of course, not their most hospitable location. Added to the perils of the weather is the threat posed by the polluted atmosphere which attacks all materials, and increasingly there is the risk of vandalism.

Damage and deterioration cannot be eliminated altogether, so the aim of conservation is to slow down the process of degradation, to preserve as much as possible, and to avoid further damage either subsequently or as a result of the conservation method. Perhaps the most useful principles to bear in mind when attempting to intervene are;

❖ conservation procedures must be reversible; *and*

❖ any intervention should be of the absolute minimum necessary to repair or maintain the object.

This article sets out the approach taken by us at Cliveden in the course of work in the repair of stone and a short account is given of the work by colleagues in the National Trust in the repair and maintenance of metals and terracotta.

It should be stated at the outset that all statuary and monuments work should only be undertaken on the personal advice of an experienced and professionally recommended conservator.

DECAY

Decay is by three means: physical, chemical or from organic growths. How great the level of decay is dependent on the location and the suitability of the material for its setting.

A granite pedestal for example, will defy the hostile weathers of a Scottish garden setting more ably than a fine French limestone, as indeed, a lead statue will be more appropriate than a sculpture cast in bronze and given a gilt finish.

Stone

All stone has a degree of porosity. The slow attrition of a stone surface by a slightly acidic rain water containing

Anglesey Abbey Gardens, Cambridgeshire
18th Century figure of Father Time is lifted for the insertion of a sound foundation and damp proof course.

sulphur dioxide and carbon dioxide not only attacks the fine carving, it will also soften and make absorption by rain and pollution more possible. Dry and wet deposits of hydrocarbons together with ozone and surrounding secondary deposits of sulphuric and nitric acids are also harmful. If stones are not washed free of acidic deposits by rainfall, then increasingly thick, dirty crusts will form on the surface. Limestones and marbles are particularly vulnerable, the encrusted surface peeling away through differential movement in hot and cold temperatures, and leading to a general deterioration of the softened surface beneath.

Such changes will make frost action more possible as the stone is made more absorbent and thus prone to freeze/thaw action in sub-zero temperatures. It is recorded that acid rain has caused more decay in stone buildings in the last 100 years than in the last 2,000. Up to 50mm of stone has been dissolved on the copings of St. Paul's Cathedral since their construction in 1760.

Iron fixings, which were often embedded in stone, will rust when damp and in the process expand greatly causing the surrounding material to crack or even shatter.

Cultures of organic growths are encouraged by a higher level of dampness, biological growths being both seen and unseen; lichen, algae and mosses lie on the surface holding moisture and producing harmful chelators of carbonic and oxalic acid among others. Hidden bacterial cultures require little moisture, retaining water themselves in the body of stone. Bacteria will fix nitrates and combine with sooty crusts to create disfiguring blemishes.

Metals
A damp and polluted environment is also a great enemy of metal sculptures. Some metals are more resistant than others, but generally corrosion occurs to all in an

outdoor setting, and in all cases, their important surface finishes or patinations are at considerable risk outdoors.

The manufacturing process of metal sculpture will often determine the cause of deterioration. Historically, casting processes have incorporated jointing, reinforcement, armatures and core work of both inappropriate and incompatible materials.

Bronze, the most common material for metal statuary, is harmed by acid precipitation; pollutants of sulphur and nitrogen oxide attack the surface, changing its appearance and damaging its structure. Such deterioration is green in colour and, because of its frequent occurrence, became accepted as the natural and preferred colour for bronzes. Consequently the protective surface patination applied by foundries sometimes incorporated a green colour. Iron was also used as reinforcement, leaving the sculpture vulnerable to rust expansion within the material and consequent damage.

Lead, although the most durable of metals commonly used, is to a degree corroded by atmospheric pollution. Its surface will be oxidised and if inadequately supported through failure of an internal armature, will be stretched to permanent distortion.

The setting up of a replica Coade Stone Borghese Urn and pedestal at Chiswick House.

Terracotta
Some of the best preserved examples of garden statuary have been manufactured in fired clay or 'terracotta'. Patented high fired stoneware such as Mrs Coade's Coade stone are more likely to remain in good condition, but low fired, more porous ceramic material is prone to frost attack and the absorption of ground salts. Terracotta has a relatively resistant surface or 'fire-skin' which provides some protection, but it is easily damaged, particularly by cleaning.

Concrete
The deterioration of cast concrete sculpture often originates at the time of its manufacture due to production faults and the corrosion of ferrous metal armatures. The use of cement based concrete statuary

popular since the middle of the 19th Century requires considerable skill and knowledge in its manufacture to be durable.

MAINTENANCE AND CONSERVATION
Regular, carefully considered maintenance and appropriate, timely repair work will prolong the life of all garden ornaments, often with the minimum of expenditure. Sadly, only recently are owners and those responsible for collections waking up to the realisation that funds for maintenance work should be allocated for monuments. Stone and metalwork, because of their apparent resistance to wear and tear are left alone and only when deterioration becomes obvious are attempts made to put things right, often too late.

Much of the blame for such oversight can be put down to both fashion and ignorance. We have a romantic notion that garden statuary and monuments should show their age and for this reason a degree of deterioration is accepted. However, the attractive mantels of lichen and moss and the staining and peeling away of a worn stone surface belie a more serious threat to the well being of the monument. In addition, the simplest procedures for the care of buildings and sculpture materials are not widely known.

Increasingly responsible bodies such as the National Trust and English Heritage are placing greater emphasis on preventative conservation. In the forefront of this approach is the maintenance programme.

Surveys and planning
The basis for all conservation programmes, including routine maintenance, is the survey by a specialist conservator. Apart from the obvious advantages of planning, surveys assist grant application and the monitoring and recording of deterioration, and a report should be produced summarising the condition of the piece, together with recommendations for repair and maintenance. The goals of both preservation and the presentation of the statuary or monument should be identified, and the report should be a true and objective statement on the condition of the piece, not a proposal for work.

Repair priorities and costs will be set out in the recommendations. Aspects of work other than technical matters will be reviewed. For example, individual pieces within a collection must be treated with the aesthetic awareness of the appearance of all the collection.

If necessary the advice of an historian should be sought on the matter of historic precedent for patination, colour schemes, decoration and setting.

Routine maintenance
Maintenance programmes look to both preserve and to monitor. It will not always be possible for a trained conservator to undertake either maintenance or monitoring and so that which is strictly an

National Trust Building Supervisor taking part in a mortar and pointing course for historic buildings and monuments at Lacock Abbey, Wiltshire

area of responsibility for a conservator must be clearly identified. Work to be undertaken by the non-specialist must be clarified and adequate instruction given. In The National Trust a training programme is under way within each Region. Led by the Regional Conservator, maintenance teams undertake regular maintenance work for all garden statuary.

The reduction of the ingress of water, the periodic removal of pollutants, the control of organic growths and the maintenance of structural integrity to both the support and the fabric of the statue and monument are all fundamental aims. Increasingly, prevention of theft, vandalism and accidental damage by traffic and changes elsewhere in the garden are matters to be addressed.

Joints, cracks and natural fissures in stonework should be monitored and pointed or filled if necessary. Pointing materials should be well chosen, and are to be of lesser strength and greater porosity than the surrounding stone and of suitable colour and texture. Lime and aggregate (never cement if at all possible) mixed to form a mortar will not only look well but will have the advantage of improving in appearance and condition with age. Metal surfaces and armatures, even if corroded, when sealed against weathering by a suitable wax, will be protected for a smooth impervious surface will assist the removal of pollutants. Application of the wax follows scrubbing with water and detergent that removes dust and acidic surface debris. The wax *(microcrystalline)* can contain a corrosive inhibitor *(benzotriazole)*.

Unfortunately a suitable sealer that will allow the free evaporation of moisture from stone is not available. However, since the late 1970s techniques of protecting limestone and marble statuary with coatings have produced treatments that are centred on the use of lime mortar. Lime is applied in the form of mortars with a sheltercoat of lime wash which, if applied thinly, can provide a tonal wash unifying a decayed and broken surface, and will assist run off of rainwater and pollution.

Organic growths in contact with the stone require controlling, although their complete removal is not always possible. Plants should be weeded out as roots not only grow larger but will encourage soil build-up. Lichen and algae growths should be inhibited to an appropriate degree by suitable strengths of biocides sprayed or brushed on.

For all outdoor statuary, isolation from ground water and the accompanying soluble salts by a damp-proof course is necessary, and is usually of lead *(code 5)*.

All stonework and metalwork requires firm foundation, corework in pedestals and sound fixings, all of which require constant monitoring for signs of decay.

The provision of winter covers for statuary is essential in order to keep them dry and minimise the risk of freeze-thaw frost action. Before the Second World War covers were an expected part of the winter scene in gardens, but their use faded out during the war and are only now reappearing. Traditionally wooden boxes of sentry-box design, more modern versions are tent-like, with alloy frames and canvas covers. Openings at base and sides keep the tents well ventilated and where weathers are particularly harsh, internal insulation is recommended.

Conservation

Where statuary or monuments are in considerable and immediate danger from decay, then repair procedures are adopted that are more radical and intervening.

Cleaning is one of the more controversial areas in conservation. If undertaken unsympathetically or indelicately, the removal of dirt can all but ruin the appearance of stone or metal and damage its fabric. Yet if undertaken

The carving of a replacement muse figure for the Orangery at Belton, Lincolnshire

sensitively, judicious dirt removal can enhance a sculpture, highlighting modelling and revealing tool marks and finishes set in to provide shading to the composition. Cleaning should be carefully planned in order to guarantee that which is unwanted is removed. As tastes in conservation become more conservative, increasingly only the bare minimum of work is called for and as our knowledge of period finishes increases, we are becoming more cautious about cleaning. Patinations are often delicate and may, in time, have become incorporated with the dirt layer.

Stonework and terracotta will benefit from gentle, regular cleaning. A little water and a brush will help to keep the pores clear of clogging dirt and polluted grime. The improvement of air abrasive techniques augmented now by laser cleaning are both methods being marketed for monument and building conservation. However the success of all cleaning methods depend on a high degree of skill and training. The surfaces of many buildings and monuments have been destroyed in the belief that a cleaned structure looks healthier.

No cleaning takes place without trials and test areas to assess its likely affect and a conservator should thoroughly inspect any surface prior to cleaning and as work commences to avoid disastrous losses of finishes.

Consolidation and surface sealants

The strengthening of decayed statuary stone using the impregnation of acrylic, epoxy and silane and other resins is a technique which has been broadened to be used on large scale stonework of monuments. This work is generally irreversible and requires the utmost care in application. The consolidation of stone can both alter its appearance and affect its permeability and porosity.

Structural repairs

If an internal frame of a sculpture or the internal fixing of a monument has failed, then replacement is often the only option. Often access is only possible by radical surgery, cutting open a sculpture or taking down a monument. Attempts to avoid such expense by the coating of the armature or fixings with rust inhibitors or grouting prove temporary, and more costly treatments are more economic in the long term.

THE LAST RESORT

In some cases when statuary is too delicate or subject to an unacceptable risk of damage in its location, the sculpture must be taken indoors for protection. The making of copies for display outdoors in their original location is increasingly becoming an option in conservation. The use of silicone resin moulds and stone dust mixes for casts makes replication convincing, and as technology is put to use in the increasing market of new garden statuary, carving by laser beam to be finished by a competent sculptor is looking increasingly affordable. ✄

TREVOR PROUDFOOT is the Managing Director of Cliveden Conservation Workshops Limited, and advisor for stone and plaster conservation to the National Trust.

New Developments in Bulb Technology for Traditional Landscapes

FRANS ROOZEN

It is possible to synchronise flowering periods very accurately with bulb varieties

BULBS have played an important part in decorative horticulture for centuries. Recently in Holland we have celebrated the 400th anniversary of the introduction of the tulip from Turkey, although one of the earliest illustrations of the flower is on a vase dated about 1600 BC and found in the palace of Minos at Knossos in Crete, although it is not known whether the multi-headed tulip depicted was cultivated in gardens.

In Europe bulbs such as daffodils and lilies had been cultivated before the tulip appeared in Holland, often featuring in monastery gardens. They did not necessarily make a major visual impact for they were regarded more as curiosities and

investments; witness the turbulence of the period of Tulipomania during the 1700s. It was not until Victorian times that bulbs became really significant for the large gardens of Europe.

Today they have a very important role to play, for not only do they provide almost every possible colour combination and characteristic, but in the strident economic times in which we find ourselves, they are amongst the most cost-effective plants to grow. Not only are establishment costs reasonable, but most important of all, their maintenance requirements can be reduced, in some instances below those of keeping an unplanted area in good order.

While there are many reasons for considering growing bulbs in an historic park or garden, the most important, if the property is open to visitors, is the ability to target a colourful spectacle to within a week or ten days of a specific date. Indeed it is unusual for any bulb to vary in its flowering period for more than a day or two providing that it was planted correctly and on time and the weather was not too uncharitable during the growing period.

This ability to create a display within a very narrow time frame is extremely important, especially at the beginning of the year. Some gardens exploit the fact that others in their locality do not open in the early part of the year and then create a snowdrop or aconite spectacular to provide a bonus opening when they would not normally be deriving any income, while more traditional owners will look to plant spring flowering varieties which will create an exciting kick-off to the season, precisely on opening day.

This latter is exceptionally important as the first experience of a property at the beginning of the season is likely to colour a visitor's view of it when considering subsequent visits. Even if the weather is appalling, if there is beauty all around, the urge to return is far greater than when confronted with gloomy grey skies and dripping foliage. It is this great ability to create a spectacle, and to do so the first season, at a pre-determined time which adds to an overall appreciation that bulbs are an economical investment.

Apart from their ability to be carefully exploited for visitor attraction and financial gain, they are truly inexpensive when placed alongside other plant material. From a practical point of view, because of their life cycle and established dormant state at planting time, they are cheaply established. Their life cycle also affects horticultural maintenance, which if carefully planned can be minimised. Pests and diseases are few and far between, rarely creating a problem; any that arise being dealt with immediately. There is no complicated on-going spraying programme necessary.

Tulips naturalised in grass are a relatively recent phenomenon

Daffodils have the ability to create a great spectacle

Top quality bulbs are necessary to provide a high quality display

Much of the success of bulb planting can be attributed to the correct selection of bulbs. The quality of bulbs is vitally important, only top quality material being used. There are no bargains amongst cheap bulbs. If you are not paying the proper price you are no doubt purchasing discarded forced bulbs which will almost certainly grow and flower, but by virtue of being cut flower varieties will not necessarily bloom when you expect and may well have heavy heads which will be flattened by prolonged rain. Bulb varieties which were used for cut flowers are unlikely to be any good for landscape planting.

Recent trials have indicated useful ways of both deciding upon the selection of suitable bulb varieties and also their subsequent management. From the point of view of longevity, work on double depth planting suggests a new way forward and has thrown up certain groups of bulbs which will respond to the technique and can now be used widely. Most narcissus, except the jonquils, respond along with the brightly coloured and extremely versatile hybrid tulips derived from *Tulipa kaufmanniana*, *T. fosteriana* and *T. greigii*. Hyacinths unfortunately are not suited to this style of management.

The recent revelation that many narcissus and tulips respond favourably to being planted at twice the normal depth creates a wealth of opportunities for using bulbs in places where they have never been considered previously. Shallow planting and the interference caused by cultivations during the summer months when the bulbs are dormant precluded their use from many mixed planting schemes. Now they can be placed beneath the reach of the fork or hoe and still perform well.

An added bonus with tulips is the extra life which double depth planting has bestowed upon them. Previously they were considered of annual duration, especially on heavy clay soils where they usually only produced a handful of foliage the second year. Now they blossom regularly and produce plenty of leaves, a potential problem after a few years as they create conditions for botrytis. Older plantings should have its emerging foliage occasionally thinned in order to permit better air circulation and reduce the likelihood of the fungal disease attacking.

Variable depth planting can also have implications with naturalised bulbs, for they can now be planted beneath the roots of competing grasses. Little is understood of the relationship between bulbs and grass, although extensive experiments by the International Flower Bulb Centre at Harlow Carr Gardens, Harrogate, are addressing the affects of various grass seed mixtures upon the performance of bulbs. It will be two or three more years before the work is complete, but at present it would seem that the fescues are the most suitable grasses for a happy relationship with bulbs.

It is with naturalised bulbs that the historic garden can really benefit, for many open grassy areas can be brightened up at little initial cost. Subsequent maintenance can also be reduced, for places which were once mown six or more times a year subsequently only require cutting on two or three occasions. Indeed some gardens now find it fashionable to arrange their naturalised bulb plantings in such a way that when the time comes for initial mowing, only swathes are taken out in places where visitors will walk, the uncut grass being cut around in such a way that it creates an additional temporary garden sculpture feature. This is not wholly in keeping with history, but in parts of the garden where there is license to experiment, it is very effective.

The International Flower Bulb Centre has recently been working on a collaborative project in Yorkshire to determine the exact costs of maintenance of naturalised areas of bulbs and grass. The final figures will not become available for another couple of seasons. However, in certain circumstances, especially in places where it is difficult and time-consuming to mow, it can already be proved beyond reasonable doubt that by reducing cutting frequency as a result of planting bulbs, that after two seasons the cost of the bulbs and their planting is recovered.

Adjusting densities can also make a marked difference to establishment costs. Instead of choosing regular single headed daffodils for example, look at the opportunities presented by multi-headed cultivars. The multi-headed *'Tête a Tête'* costs about half as much again as its contemporaries, but it can be planted at a third the density. It is true that without regular lifting the ability to produce multi-flowered heads diminishes, but not any quicker than the increase in bulb numbers. So as one declines the other increases and the floral display remains consistent.

New developments with the dwarf growing tulips gives the garden manager another option for bulb naturalising. Rarely ever tried in grass and seldom succeeding well, tulips have largely been ignored by planters. Recent work with cultivars of *Tulip kaufmanniana* and the introduction of *'Scarlet Baby'* have changed all this. *'Scarlet Baby'* is especially versatile, being an early flowered tulip which naturalises and forms clumps, rather like daffodils. Its contemporaries are not quite as prolific, but are certainly worth considering for a late March or early April display.

It may be thought that the use of tulips in this way in an historic garden is questionable as this is a distinctly 1990s development. However, their appearance, providing cultivars like *'Heart's Delight'* are used, is subtle enough to associate well with aged trees and old buildings and creates the ambience of earlier times. Unlike the fabric of a period house, we also have to remember that much of the fabric of a garden changes with the seasons and the natural cycle of decay and renewal is vital to its interest and enjoyment. ✷

Frans Roozen is the technical director of the International Flower Bulb Centre, Hillegom, Holland (telephone 00 31 2520 15254) and is responsible for the provision of technical information upon the cultivation of bulbs to gardeners and growers throughout the world. He is a world-renowned authority who has written many articles and papers on bulbs and their cultivation.

ENSURING THE CONTINUITY OF PARKLAND TREES

CLIVE PARKER

ONE of the finest features of our historic parks and landscapes is the trees. Although seemingly timeless landscape features they demand regular and skilled attention if they are to retain their unique character. Maturity is the greatest problem, for most of our stock of parkland trees is now mature, a condition which with most species can remain stable for between fifty and a hundred years.

The park or garden manager must have a long term view of the health of his tree stock and take remedial action whenever it is necessary. Trees are long suffering and visually tolerant of neglect, as has been amply proven in the recent recession when on many estates no routine tree work was carried out because of financial constraints.

Nevertheless this should not be allowed to continue or we will recreate the conditions just after the last war when the neglect of parkland trees led to great losses in our landscape. While maintenance can often be delayed for twelve to eighteen months without serious consequence, longer periods of neglect can lead to disaster.

Assessing the condition of trees demands an expert eye and so a periodic inspection by an arboricultural specialist is a good investment. If this is undertaken every three or four years any potentially serious problem can be nipped in the bud.

However, the competent park manager can spot many potential problems well ahead of time and then take appropriate action to remedy them. He may need specialist advice about the exact cause of the symptoms, but the symptoms themselves can be readily discerned with the practised eye.

Stag heading of trees is one of the most frequent signs that all is not well. It is a condition which can arise from a number of causes, but in recent years has largely resulted from the drought conditions prevalent in many parts of the country. A very descriptive term, stag heading is when the crowns of trees lose many of their leaves and the naked branches stand out against the sky from amongst a leafy canopy.

Vivid foliage colours at any time of the year should be regarded with suspicion. Only trees that normally colour in the autumn should be considered healthy, and

Careful bracing using modern techniques can prolong the life of a tree

All photos provided by the author.

only when the entire tree colours consistently and at the same time. Any branches that colour prematurely, or do so on a tree that is not noted for its colour, should be carefully inspected.

Premature aging is often the result of some impediment to nutrient or moisture uptake and can indicate the presence of a fungal disease. Alternatively it may be caused by mechanical means, such as an over-tight brace or tie which is constricting development of the branch.

Weeping from any part of the tree should be regarded with suspicion. This may be the result of mechanical damage, a fungal rot or even attack by bacterial disease. This latter would produce a sticky exudation, often accompanied by the dying back of young shoots and the blackening of foliage.

Any fungal growth either on the tree or around the base particularly must give cause for concern. Bracket fungi of various kinds usually indicate imminent decay and while some of the toadstool-like parasols growing around the base of the tree, may be perfectly innocuous, they may equally well indicate an attack by the honey fungus. Unless a fungal presence can be

readily identified, and if necessary treated to prevent damage to the tree, expert advice should be sought. A skilled arborist should be able to provide a diagnosis of the problem and determine the extent of the damage. This may be done using a borer to remove a sample, although increasingly modern sounding and scanning techniques are being used to determine tissue damage without physical investigation.

With regular inspections few unexpected surprises occur, which in turn ensures smooth trouble-free management. However, management is not only about

Trees often require weight to be taken out of their canopies in order to withstand severe autumn gales

spotting trouble when it occurs and dealing with it properly, it is much more about consistent care.

Once a tree population has been brought up to a good standard an on-going maintenance programme should be implemented. Nowadays using computerised systems like Ezy Treev, it is possible to bring together documentation, mapping and management into a simple to operate programme which can be easily and regularly updated.

Mature trees require regular pruning to remove dead and dying wood from both an aesthetic and safety point of view. The regular cutting out of faded branches ensures that die back does not occur beyond that which is natural and harmless.

Trees often require some of the weight taking out of their canopy to enable them to cope with severe autumn gales, while there is also often a need to raise crowns in order to permit operations such as grass cutting beneath. Such routine pruning also enables careful observation of the condition of individual trees to be made in a quite intimate way.

This also ensures advance warning of the need to support and brace trees. With

careful bracing using modern techniques the life of many individuals can be lengthened. Unlike the clumsy and unsightly methods of yesteryear, present day systems are largely unobtrusive but equally effective.

Preserving mature trees is obviously critical, but preparing to replace them is vital. There is no easy method in landscape terms of ensuring continuity, for two wars have largely disrupted the continued development of the tree-scape in our parks and landscapes. Decisions have to be made about inter-planting and grouping amongst the existing tree stock, which may not be visually appropriate, or taking an adjacent area to re-establish a parkland, completely obliterating the existing park when the trees are beyond redemption.

This latter route damages the historic interest of the landscape by changing its design, but may be unavoidable. It is the most effective method of re-establishing a shattered landscape. It also enables a workable management policy for the next century, and beyond, to be established with every expectation of continuity being achieved and the problems of the last century avoided.

Such decisions cannot be made in a general way, each manager and owner having to come to terms with his individual situation. However, something has to be done.

The next dilemma is the type of plant material that is used. Not only the planting size, but the provenance as well must be considered.

By and large parkland trees are species of local origin. Do we continue down this road, or should we look to modern cultivars or selections from species which may not be of local origin, but of similar appearance but with perhaps improved disease resistance or wider tolerance of soil conditions? Again this is a personal decision for the owner and manager, but one which should not be dismissed lightly.

Deciding the size of stock to plant is another matter of personal choice. It is quite possible to use modern machinery to successfully lift and transplant trees up to thirty feet high. After care is crucial, especially staking and watering, the latter often being necessary for three years or so until the trees are well established. However most arborists will agree that smaller trees establish more quickly and are easier to maintain, in many cases catching semi-mature plantings up in very few years. The advantage of semi-mature introductions is the instant effect, although in many cases the cost is likely to be prohibitive. ✄

Clive Parker has extensive practical experience in the management of amenity trees. He trained at the Royal Botanic Gardens, Kew and worked for local authorities, and the National Trust before becoming the Head of Arboriculture and forestry at Houghall College, Durham.

SALTWELL PARK GATESHEAD

JOHN PENDLEBURY and ALISON CAMPBELL

THE park lies in an area developed in the 19th Century with the houses of prosperous Tyneside industrialists and forms the heart of the Saltwell Conservation Area. It provides a major open space for dense urban housing to the north and a demonstration of the civic pride of the town of Gateshead.

The development of the park was an inspired piece of opportunism. The park was superimposed on the estate of the prominent stained glass manufacturer William Wailes, who had built himself a romantic polychromatic brick villa, Saltwell Towers, with a complex garden using retaining walls as castellated belvederes and incorporating a natural dene or valley as a picturesque approach to the house. Shortly after its construction Wailes fell into financial difficulties, and the estate was taken over to provide a municipal park. The layout of the park is attributed to Edward Kemp. In the southern section this involved modest adaptations to Wailes' ambitious garden. Kemp enhanced the circulation and through planting skilfully inserted enclosed spaces for formal games such as bowls and quoits. In the northern section open fields were incorporated as parkland using a more conventional municipal park plan. This area has strong peripheral tree planting and sinuous paths and tree clumps. Along the upper side is a formal promenade broadwalk terminated by two rustic shelters and at its centre a pavilion which has an axial view down to a large irregularly shaped lake. Subsequent changes have included an extension of 1920 to incorporate Saltwell Grove house and garden to the south and the introduction of new activity spaces which, until the 1960s at least, were mostly successful and complementary.

The great cultural legacy of the Victorian Municipal Park has rightly attracted much interest over recent years. Publications such as 'People's Parks' by Hazel Conway outline the great social, political and historic value of parks as well as their significance in the development of designed landscapes. Conversely 'Public Prospects, Historic Urban Parks Under Threat' published by the Victorian Society and the Garden History Society has demonstrated the pressures and threats that face the public park. The report illustrates parks with phenomenal problems of

A postcard view of Saltwell Towers in 1900

Saltwell Park is a very popular traditional park with bedding displays, bowls, boating, events and well used areas for informal recreation. It is also a fine example of a 19th Century municipal park and is included in the English Heritage Register of Parks and Gardens of Special Historic Interest.
In recent years good decorative planting and routine maintenance have tended to obscure serious underlying problems, including redundant and dilapidated buildings, poor structural 'management', and a loss of important views.
JOHN PENDLEBURY and ALISON CAMPBELL describe current proposals to ensure its future.

A similar view today, showing how a lack of proper management has affected important historic views

vandalism, arson and theft. Elsewhere hard strapped local authorities are selling off chunks of parks for development, often for uses such as leisure centres and garden centres. Superficially these can appear compatible with a park but often they erode both its historic character and its value as open space.

Despite some apparent problems, (the centre-piece building Saltwell Towers has been a shell for many years), Saltwell Park displays little sign of the dramatic threats described by 'Public Prospects'. However, Saltwell illustrates that traditional management, on site park-keepers and horticultural staff keeping a tidy decorative appearance, combined with high visitor numbers, can belie serious problems.

Three factors underlie most of these problems, which are typical of many other Victorian parks. Firstly, in some instances maintenance has failed to keep pace with necessary repairs to fabric. For example, the failure over many years to recognise the need for regular replanting within the landscape framework has resulted in a tree stock of uniform age, which is reaching a critical stage of over-maturity. The recent loss of over four hundred elm trees is only

The belvedere walls around Saltwell Towers

the tip of a major problem. Another example is provided by Saltwell Towers which was closed as a museum in 1968 as it needed, at that stage, relatively modest repairs. As these were not undertaken the building deteriorated rapidly to the point where it is now a roofless shell. Secondly, problems can be caused where areas and features have lost their original function. The pavilion on the broadwalk, for example, which was originally a tearoom,

had stood empty for a number of years. The vulnerability of unused buildings was shown when the pavilion was severely damaged by arsonists in 1993. Crucial to discussions over restoration has been the issue of finding a use for the building. Similarly, changing circulation patterns had led to the lower part of the dene becoming less frequented and led to a perception that the area needed a new role; the result was a well intentioned but poor quality 'enhancement' using a job creation scheme. Thirdly, a lack of appreciation of historic significance has led in places to inappropriate additions and repairs and to a loss of important views. These problems led Gateshead Council to put forward a bid in June 1994 for English Heritage Conservation Area Partnership funding.

English Heritage Conservation Area Partnership (CAP) is a new approach to conservation area funding in England. It is intended to target resources more effectively in order to solve problems in an area, rather than to drip feed individual, often isolated projects over a long period of time. From 1995 CAPs will be phased in to become the main means by which English Heritage

The axial view from the broad walk to the lake.

The lake; damaged edging and poor quality guard rail detract from its appearance.

A high quality of decorative feature belies serious structural problems, such as the loss of trees.

financially supports works in conservation areas. In order for a scheme to qualify for assistance, it will be necessary to show that the conservation area, or the part of the area concerned, is of a demonstrable quality and also that there are significant problems which warrant grant assistance. This seemed very suited to tackling the problems of Saltwell Park, enabling a holistic approach which considers the park as a whole and complex entity rather than the setting for a number of discreet structures.

The English Heritage Register of Parks and Gardens established the principle that designed landscapes are more than the built structures they contain. However, in preparing a bid for Conservation Area Partnership, funded by an organisation more familiar with schemes for buildings, the case for park conservation had to be carefully explained. Recent debates in garden history circles over possible statutory control in historic parks and gardens have focused on a distinction between structural and decorative elements. This methodology was adopted as a means of assessing the park and illustrating what is of importance in the designed landscape. Structural elements might for example, include a belt of trees which define space and provide character, and are just as important to the structure of the park as a wall performing the same function. Similarly the lake in Saltwell Park is as important as a focal point in the parkland as the pavilion which faces

it along the central axial vista. Decorative elements are those considered as embellishments of a more transitory nature such as floral displays of bedding plants. The precise application of the terms can be debated but this approach allows living elements of the park to be assessed on an equal footing with traditional architectural elements.

In addition to demonstrating the quality of the area, the application for CAP required an outline of problems, a listing of grant-eligible works with cost estimates and a phasing programme. The assessment needed to be a multi-disciplinary approach using the skills of a number of Council departments. Though this involved much new work, it also drew on surveys and reviews over the last ten years. Importantly some steps had recently been taken in the right direction; for example the Tyne and Wear Building Preservation Trust had been grant aided to undertake a feasibility study on Saltwell Towers. The structural problems of the park were considered under the following headings:

❖ design of space, elements that define and provide character to space,
❖ focal features, these range from monuments and a maze through to large features such as the lake and Saltwell Towers,
❖ infrastructure of the park, elements that perform a basic function such as paths and the drainage system,
❖ inappropriate additions, such as a 1960s

bandstand and new tree planting which has blocked vistas.

English Heritage have now agreed the principle of the partnership bid, though detailed discussions have yet to take place over what works will be eligible for assistance. The next stage is to produce a detailed Action Plan which in the case of Saltwell Park will essentially take the form of a Management Plan. This will perform a number of functions. At one level it will provide a policy framework for repair and restoration works and against which new uses and activities can be assessed. At the other extreme it will need to provide detailed specifications which can be incorporated in the Compulsory Competitive Tendering process. It is vital that the park is managed so that its many qualities are maintained, which, despite the park's problems, are still very evident today. Saltwell Park has been a source of civic pride for over 100 years and, with the help of English Heritage, Gateshead Council intends for it to stay that way for many years to come. ▓

Alison Campbell is a Landscape Architect with Gateshead Council.
John Pendlebury is Conservation Officer with Gateshead Council and co-ordinator of a North East Historic Parks and Gardens Group.

Views expressed are those of the authors and not necessarily Gateshead Council's.

PUBLIC AMENITIES FOR HISTORIC PARKS AND GARDENS

ORAN CAMPBELL

Approaching a beautiful or historic place should be like going to a musical or theatrical performance; you should arrive without your thought processes being jolted off course by obviously anachronistic or clashing sights or sounds. Visitor facilities should be discreet and fitted to the particular character of the site, not a detriment to it. ORAN CAMPBELL highlights some of the principal areas of concern and suggests some solutions.

St Augustines Abbey, Canterbury
Introductory panels designed to be seen against the chequerwork precinct wall

THE brief for each visitor facility will stem from the estimated number of visitors, the number per minute arriving at each location, and their period of stay. It might be reasonable to design for say two-thirds of peak numbers. However, if the very thing that the visitors have come to see is not to be spoilt, it may be necessary to determine an upper limit for the number of visitors invited in at any one time. Above a certain number, grass walks for example, may have to become hard paths, eroding the natural beauty or historic appearance of the place.

Adverts and leaflets should state how to recognise the entrance or illustrate it, to reduce the dependency on signage. The ideal attraction clearly indicates when one is approaching the place and has an obvious entrance. Highway authorities will often resist direction signs and if more really are needed, the Tourist Board may be able to advise.

The safety of people entering the site is vital. If the entrance could cause accidents or traffic delays, increased use may be denied by the highways authority. They may also insist on standard lighting signs and bollards at the entrance, but after this visitors should leave urban trappings behind. The entrance road and car park are a most important part of the visit and should be designed accordingly, with natural gravel surfaces and without kerbs if possible. To prevent cars straying on to grass, consider a gentle bank with a shallow ditch beyond, as at Syon Park.

The car park should be designed to reflect the particular character of the place and are best hidden by woodland, hedges or walls. It may be possible to break the parking provision into screened groups, while in formal landscapes trees can be pleached over the cars – but not English Limes! Surfaces may be part gravel with part grass for parking during peak summer use, as at The Saville Garden near Windsor. Tarmac can be dressed with suitable local gravel. Small grit will be less likely to work loose, provided that it is laid competently, in the right weather.

If it is necessary to charge for car parking, payment on entry should be avoided as it is not welcoming, could block the road, and involves notices, kiosks and other unsightly equipment at the entrance. Car flaps, on the other hand, are noisy, and pay barriers can break down needing immediate attention. Pay-and-display is preferable but does require staff to check and follow up non-payers. Rural sites may afford free parking, avoiding the need for unsightly kerbs, notices and machines. People may want to picnic, so why not design a sheltered sunny area – possibly near the car park.

Paths can often be avoided by giving wide grass areas and visible destinations,

encouraging visitors to spread out. Where they are required, modern surface and edging materials may conflict with the character of the landscape. Where kerbs are necessary to protect garden paths, only their vertical face need be visible. Steel edges are good for manicured lawns but can damage car tyres. The needs of the less able should also be considered. Thick gravel, for example, is impassable for wheelchairs. You should consult your local authority ACCESS officer for advice on visitor routes, steps and ramps.

The major facilities, including ticket sales, shop, lavatories and catering can be sited at the car park leaving the site unspoilt, as at Leeds Castle or as proposed at Stonehenge. If they are to be placed inside they must be designed to fit the place, with rigorous quality management.

Smaller sites may only need a ticket office with guide books and limited sales items. Even this place must comply with the Offices, Shops and Railway Premises Act for size, warmth etc., and the staff must have WCs, tea making and washing facilities. Here, visitors also need shelter from wind and rain and a shelf to open handbags at the very least, and the sales windows should not face the sun as visitors and staff will not see each other and displays will fade.

Lavatories should be near where staff can supervise and regularly check them as their appearance and cleanliness will convey more to visitors than even the best marketing. They should incorporate a dry, heated store for paper and cleaning materials, and somewhere to change nappies is always appreciated.

Before they explore the place, people need to know what is available, where, and what the site is about. A stand of panels can do this but beware of the puddle that will form in front! Outdoor panels deteriorate, so spare sets should be kept to hand for prompt substitution. However, the best methods of conveying information do not scatter signs over the site. Background information and history can be conveyed by guide book or an initial exhibition indoors. Best for battlefield sites is a sound and slide show that leaves mental images one can take out into the landscape and think about in peace. Tape or radio guides are effective but electronics fail in damp conditions, and it is best to have an exhibition of panels near the entrance to use when there is a breakdown.

Direction signs also add clutter, and ideally the site should be designed so that none are needed. Paths alone often suffice and should be designed so that visitors feel that they have a choice. The more spread out they are, the more people the site will comfortably take. Where essential, quickly manufactured signs are best, as replacements may be needed quickly.

Different landscapes need different fences. Split chestnut looks good in rural Sussex and dry stone walls in the North, while metal rails may suit a 19th Century domestic park. Wire fences can be discreet if seen against the light below horizon, while green wire shows up more than black. Gates should be self-closing, with a chain, counter weight and latches, and designed for wheelchair users. On roads, cattle grids can be noisy but effective, and should incorporate a hedgehog escape pipe.

The needs of people with sore joints, pregnant mothers and the elderly should also be born in mind. If properly designed, seats can be an asset in the landscape, but they can also be an eyesore, and a log, low wall, or rock may be all that is required. However, remember the grass mower when siting them.

Legally, visitors to a site are invited into a "place of undertaking" which includes all the grounds, and the management is responsible for measures to protect their

Garden furniture at Warwick Castle
Individual designs contribute individual character

health and safety. Ensure pavings, board walks, or timber bridges do not become slippery, and where there is a sheer drop of over 600mm, bear in mind that a safety rail of 1100mm height will normally be called for. On a new bridge this is possible, but on an Ancient Monument it can be a problem. If in real difficulty consult the Safety Officer at Cadw, English Heritage or Historic Scotland. Management arrangements can also provide solutions.

The staff are the managers' best allies. They need warm, ventilated, comfortable accommodation including a mess room with sink and kettle and a place to dry wet clothes. They also need staff lavatories, separate from visitors' lavatories; an office room and a place to treat people who need first aid; a telephone; a dry secure sales store; and a safe for takings.

Even contractors need shelter, storage, electricity, lavatories and parking. A designated place for grass cuttings and leaves will avoid vital areas being ruined, and a proper compost system is best. Burning areas should be carefully chosen. Large vehicles will need to come in and out from the main road without causing damage. Communications should be easy from the working areas, and the compound should be secure, and ideally screened. The one in St. James Park, London for example, is hardly noticed.

The works compound, the catering facilities, shops and tickets sales will generate litter and will need their own litter bins under the eye and responsibility of the specified staff. Other bins are usually not required. If they are emptied each night they will not be scavenged by animals. As in all these areas, not only design but also maintenance is of paramount importance.

Kenilworth Castle car park fence and bridge
Design of new facilities or railings can emphasise rural or urban character

Oran Campbell was a Regional Architect for English Heritage sites open to the public for 9 1/2 years. He instigated the first researched restoration and presentation of historic landscapes in State care, co-operating with Elizabeth Banks. He now runs Broadway Malyan Conservation, Architects; telephone 01932 845599

THE SELECTION OF TURF AND ITS MANAGEMENT IN HISTORIC GARDENS

JOHN GREGORY

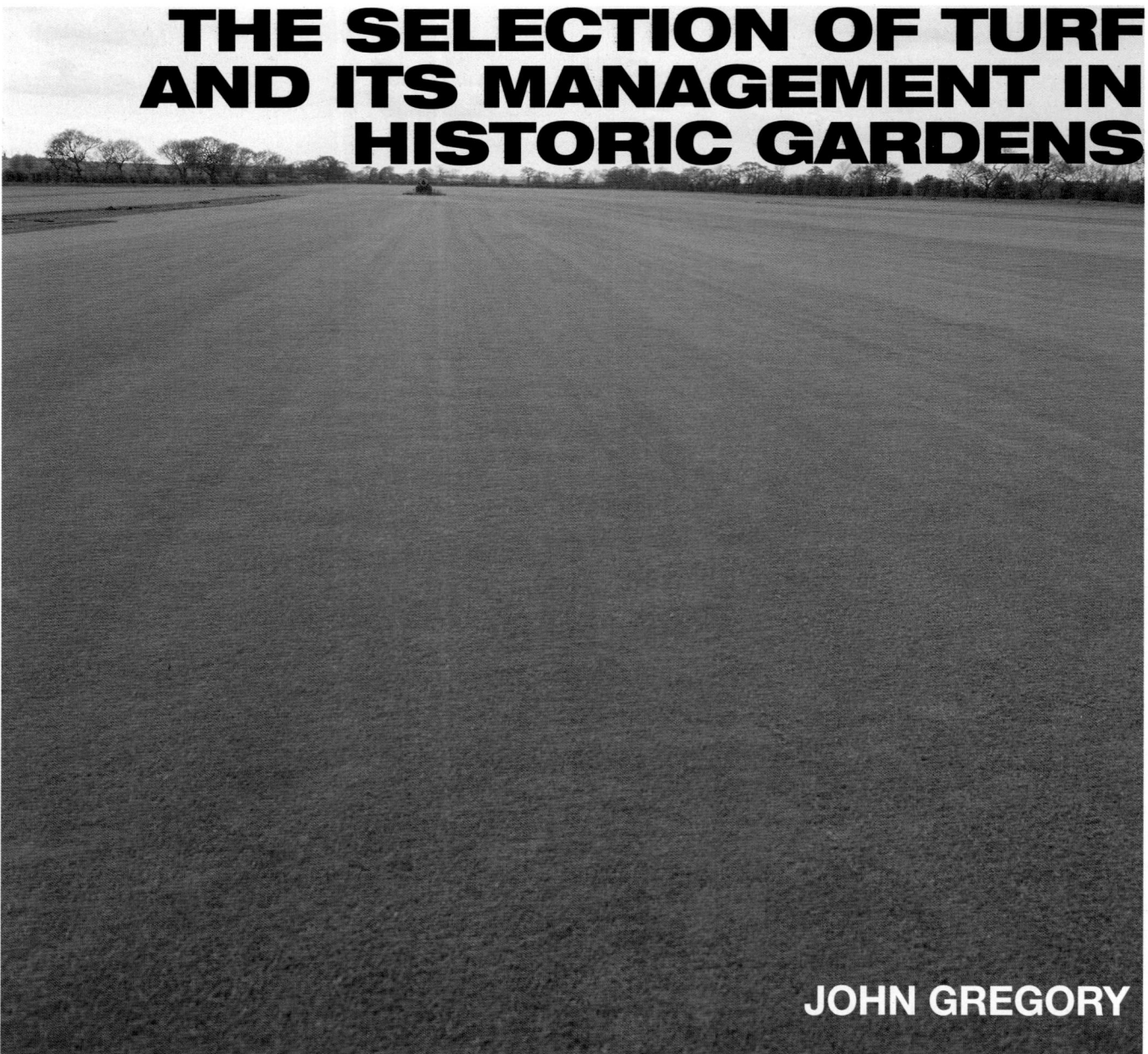

Modern field produced turf comprises very specific grass mixtures

LAWNS have been an important part of gardens for centuries, although it is only in comparatively recent times that the well mown and manicured sward has come into its own. It was the invention of the lawn mower by Edwin Budding in 1830 that created the lawn as we know it today.

Until then grassed areas had been scythed by hand. Earlier in Elizabethan times they were rarely cut, the sward being widely infiltrated by flowers – the so-called flowery mead. The advent of the modern lawn did not see an immediate improvement in grasses. This has only taken place this century and is a matter of interest to all those who now manage historic gardens. Achieving an appearance which is contemporary with the period of the house and yet tolerant of public pressure is a major consideration. Modern tolerant varieties can be used, which retain the diversity of texture typical of a pre-twentieth century lawn.

The problem with many modern grass seed mixtures is that they produce a lawn that is of too perfect an appearance for its surroundings. The kind of lawn commonly seen pictured on the front of seed catalogues is not a lawn that rests easily with Georgian or Victorian buildings. It is ideal for the formal and perfect semi-detached house garden, but when considered for an historic garden it is necessary to mix in quantities of more traditional species in order to tone down the colour intensity and perfection.

A typical high class seed of turf mixture is likely to contain 80% chewings fescue and 20% browntop bent. On acidic soils with a pH of 5.5 to 6.0 some of the chewings fescue can be replaced with slender creeping fescue, the resulting sward being strengthened by its addition. However, such a grass mixture will not take significant wear and tear and will need quite a high degree of maintenance to

ensure that it retains its purity and is not invaded by coarse native grasses and broad leafed weeds.

A hard wearing lawn should contain a high proportion of rhizomatous grasses. Typical utility mixtures contain ryegrass, smooth stalked meadow grass, chewings fescue and creeping red fescue. The proportions are variable, but for a lawn that is intended to appear high quality no more than 20% of the mixture should consist of perennial ryegrass. If a coarser appearance is desired, then the quantity of perennial ryegrass can be increased to 35–40%. This will give a very distinctive perennial ryegrass aspect, but not one that should cause any disquiet, for modern perennial ryegrass cultivars no longer leave tiresome wiry stalks in the turf after mowing.

With large areas of lawn to prepare, the historic garden manager is often able to arrange for a mixture to be created by the seedsman which will fulfil his or her

Traditional small roll turf being lifted. This is still widely used by historic gardens.

Big roll technology enables a newly laid lawn to be useable within two to three weeks.

particular requirement. The mixture can be prepared in several ways, the grasses being blended at sowing time. This means that in grassed areas where there is shade, as well as full open sunshine and perhaps specific areas of hard wear, mixtures can be selected as appropriate and by blurring the edges and blending while sowing, in time discrepancies in their appearance can be disguised.

As already indicated, perennial ryegrass is one of the most important species where the lawn is likely to take really heavy wear. Modern cultivars are visually more appealing, generally exhibiting greater disease resistance and also have a close mowing tolerance. Many have such fine leaves that some older gardeners find it difficult to believe that they are truly perennial ryegrass.

To create a fine turf with the same high degree of wear tolerance as perennial ryegrass, use modern cultivars of smooth stalked meadow grass in the mixture. These have a better tolerance of close mowing than perennial ryegrass, but are very slow to establish compared with other grasses. Once firmly established they are very resilient, recovering quickly after excessive wear and short periods of drought.

For a top quality lawn where there is unlikely to be heavy foot traffic the fescues are ideal. However, creeping red fescues do not tolerate really close mowing in the same way as chewings fescues. Both produce a quality sward which is also ideal for the naturalising of both wild flowers and bulbs. Although visually satisfactory, the growth of the fescues is such that it does not impede the development of companion plants.

Shade is often problematical, and although there are a number of tolerant species, the most useful for difficult dry areas beneath trees are the red and chewings fescues. Where conditions are moist and shady, perhaps beside walls and high buildings fine fescues and bents are more appropriate. The browntop bent *Highland* is quick to establish and develops rapidly.

For a high quality lawn, professional advice is essential. Both seed and turf suppliers are able to provide sound guidance based upon modern scientific knowledge. This advice should extend beyond the establishment stage of the lawn into routine maintenance, for different feeding regimes will benefit various grass mixtures in different ways. With the assistance of technical background information the modern head gardener or garden manager can maintain a high quality, trouble-free sward without too much difficulty.

When developing or replacing a lawn there is considerable controversy over whether seed should be sown or turf used. Cost is obviously a major consideration, but so is authenticity; for turf, because of commercial considerations, cannot be produced in such a diversity of grass mixtures as is possible with seed. However, establishment from seed not only takes longer, but is fraught with problems which turf does not encounter.

One of the greatest disadvantages with the use of seed is the high degree of labour input in both soil preparation and initial maintenance. When placed against the relatively low labour costs associated with turfing there is relatively little difference in establishment costs per square yard after the first year. The turf brings with it not only top quality grass, but also some additional soil, which in many cases makes a significant difference to lawn development, even though modern turf uses shallower rooting grasses and the soil component is only half of what it was even ten years ago.

The establishment period before the lawn is exposed to wear, to some extent determines whether seed or turf is used. A seed-raised lawn is rarely capable of receiving much foot traffic during its first year, whereas modern turf laying methods permit almost immediate use of the lawn. Although beyond the capabilities of the head gardener or garden manager laying turf by the big roll method has revolutionised lawn establishment. Each roll is 29 inches wide by 30 yards long and ¾ inch thick, often weighing in excess of a ton. This is laid by a small tracked machine with two operators. Of course it is still possible to buy conventional turf in 1 by 3 feet lengths for laying by garden staff, but if the labour input is costed, then it is often more economical to ask a contractor to lay big roll turf by machine. A further advantage is that the fewer joints there are between turves, the less likely there is to be shrinkage.

For the greatest authenticity a seed raised sward is unquestionably the most satisfactory. However, if hard wear and imminent use is desired there is no alternative but to use turf. The greatest problem with turf is its look of perfection. If this does give a cause for concern, then ask to visit a crop in the field and select that which is of the most appropriate appearance yourself, for it will look much the same once re-established as it does in the field. ▨

John Gregory trained in plant science, plant pathology and turf science. Currently the general manager of Nickerson's Turf Ltd (telephone 01673 842500), he is also an affiliate representative of the British Association of Landscape industries.

GARDEN

SIR THOMAS INGILBY

ALL current evidence points to the fact that the theft of garden ornaments, sculpture and furniture in the UK is largely organised on a commission basis. The fact that only a small percentage of stolen articles are recovered points to a strong export trade, the articles being shipped out by container. The theft of such articles has become almost endemic, with no region of the UK spared – the number of cases during the last five years runs into the hundreds. Size only represents a logistical challenge: the weight of some of the statues stolen can be measured in tonnes and a huge cast iron siege cannon stolen in Scotland soon found its way to London. Some of the sculptures lost were worth tens of thousands of pounds and with even the commonly-found wrought iron urns worth £300–£400 each, the thefts of such items has become big business. These are difficult items to protect and provided that the thief has his logistics planned, the chances of a successful raid are high.

There is a mass of evidence to show that the end collection and disposal of these stolen items is undertaken by a few 'godfathers' who commonly deal in other stolen fine art and antiques, and know their markets well. They are believed to commission thefts on a nationwide basis, the work being carried out by local criminals; gangs of three or four men are required to handle these bulky articles. These gangs work either from local knowledge or with information gleaned from the various annual stately home handbooks. The areas covered are huge: one such network, organised from central Lancashire, planned and commissioned thefts from the central Highlands of Scotland to the Isle of Wight.

Good rewards are offered to the local operatives: a man arrested recently in connection with a number of offences claimed to have been offered the sum of five thousand pounds to carry out the theft of four specific items from the grounds of a well-known stately home in southern England. Parks and gardens, cemeteries and office frontages are equally productive targets and the thieves recognise that modern sculptures can fetch just as much as their antique counterparts.

The problems of organising a defensive strategy are numerous and it has to be said that unless the items that you are defending are very close to a house that is permanently manned, your chances of achieving a foolproof system are negligible, but this doesn't mean that you cannot make life much more difficult for the thieves.

SECURITY

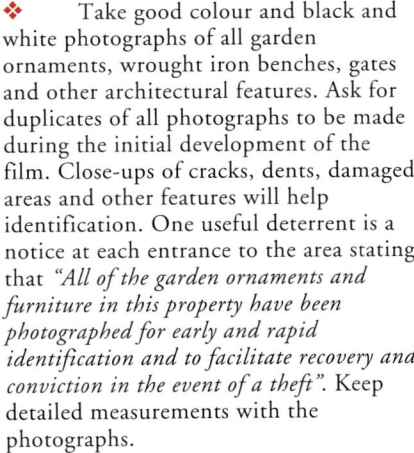

Above and top right: Access control retractable security posts. (Photos provided by VPSP Security Products)

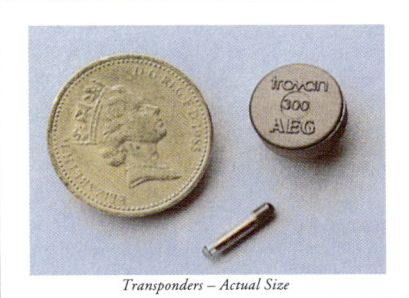

Transponders – Actual Size

The small size of transponders allows easy insertion with a few basic tools and a steady hand.
(Photo provided by Matsui Machinery Sales (UK) Ltd)

❖ Take good colour and black and white photographs of all garden ornaments, wrought iron benches, gates and other architectural features. Ask for duplicates of all photographs to be made during the initial development of the film. Close-ups of cracks, dents, damaged areas and other features will help identification. One useful deterrent is a notice at each entrance to the area stating that *"All of the garden ornaments and furniture in this property have been photographed for early and rapid identification and to facilitate recovery and conviction in the event of a theft"*. Keep detailed measurements with the photographs.

❖ Do not allow any photographs to be published which show the statues, urns etc. in your park or garden: this applies equally to annual publications and your own leaflets and brochures.

❖ Securing statues by using stainless steel pitons fixed in concrete or resin anchors may prevent their removal, but beware; many items fixed in this manner have been smashed by thieves during clumsy attempts to remove them.

❖ Thieves usually rely on wheelbarrows etc. found on site to transport the property. Treat your implement store as a potential arsenal for thieves and protect it accordingly.

❖ Secure all access gates, but remember that padlock and chain are soon defeated by bolt cutters unless case-hardened steel chain is used. To prevent gates being lifted off their hinges insert a semi-circular metal bracket through the gates and bed it into the wall or gatepost on either side, like a staple.

❖ Dig flower beds (preferably roses) around statues/urns. Soft earth leaves footprints and inconveniences the thieves using wheelbarrows. Roses scratch and again cause problems for wheelbarrows.

❖ If anything is particularly vulnerable, i.e. it is valuable and light enough for two or three men to lift, my advice would be to remove it indoors for safe keeping. It is possible to commission a very authentic looking original that will pass all but the closest scrutiny. Check with your local planning officer first if the items concerned are listed or in a listed garden or conservation area, since you may require Listed Building consent move them.

❖ Access routes and gateways can be guarded very effectively by blocking them with telescopic anti-ram raid devices. If thieves cannot get a vehicle close to the ornaments (and don't forget field gate access points that lead into the park or adjacent fields) they will have great difficulty in getting the items away. These bollards disappear into recesses in the ground when not in use but once locked into place, will stop anything up to a twenty ton truck.

❖ External 'movement or heat detection' lighting is very effective where power sources are available nearby; it can come complete with a warning message delivered once the device is activated. *"You are in a prohibited zone – please leave immediately or the police will be notified"* – or words to that effect.

❖ Ensure that all garden staff and stewards are aware of the threat of theft; encourage them to make a note of all suspicious characters – those who try to enter private areas or spend rather too much time examining the ornaments or who just don't look like bona fide visitors. Descriptions of suspects and their vehicles are invaluable and can be quickly checked by local police.

❖ Dogs and guinea fowl can be good alarms when disturbed by intruders.

❖ Note the serial number of all your garden mowers, chain saws and strimmers: could you positively identify yours if three identical machines were placed side by side? If you can't, you may not get it back. Use an ultra violet pen to mark your postcode on all machines and tools and renew all the markings regularly. Take expert advice from the pen's manufacturer that no substance in the pen will damage the property that you are marking; porcelain, for instance, can be damaged by this process.

❖ Various firms have devised alarms to protect garden ornaments and the technology is now quite reliable. Only the more valuable statues are likely to qualify for what is still quite costly treatment, and you have to ask yourself: "if the alarm does go off at 2.00 a.m., who is going to race outside in the dark to confront a gang of hefty men in the garden?"

❖ It is possible to get thumbnail sized transponders, each with a unique identification number, which can be implanted in statues etc. These can subsequently be detected by scanners held by regional police forces to detect motorbike theft. ✺

SIR THOMAS INGILBY is the owner of Ripley Castle, near Harrogate in North Yorkshire.

The castle and its walled gardens are open to the public on a regular basis and in 1988 he founded the National Stately Home Hotline, an organisation which helps its membership (now over five hundred strong) to keep up-to-date with the latest intelligence on thefts inside and outside historic properties.

FOR FURTHER INFORMATION

KEY ORGANISATIONS

ARBORICULTURAL ADVISORY AND INFORMATION SERVICE
Alice Holt Lodge, Wrecclesham, Farnham, Surrey GU10 4LH
Tel 01420 22022
The Service aims to develop the highest standards of amenity tree management by publishing up-to-date information and providing advice. Arboricultural research notes are available.

ARBORICULTURAL ASSOCIATION
Ampfield House, Ampfield, Romsey, Hampshire SO51 9PA
Tel 01794 368717

THE ASSOCIATION OF GARDEN TRUSTS
Cadland House, Fawley, Southampton SO4 1AA
Tel 01306 611268

ASSOCIATION OF LANDSCAPE MANAGEMENT
38 Highfield Drive, Birstall, Batley, West Yorkshire WF17 9BG
Tel 01924 470292

BOTANIC GARDENS CONSERVATION INTERNATIONAL
Desacano House, 199 Kew Road, Richmond, Surrey TW9 3BW
Tel 0181 332 5953/4
Botanic Gardens Conservation International is an international network of botanic gardens dedicated to plant conservation. It is registered as a UK charity. BGCI assists in the redevelopment of many historic botanic gardens acting as a centre for co-ordination, technical support and advice.

BOTANICAL SOCIETY OF THE BRITISH ISLES
c/o Department of Botany, Natural History Museum, Cromwell Road, London SW7 5BD
Tel 0171 938 8701
The Society offers the leaflet 'Growing Wild Flowers from Seed' free for s.a.e. from above address. 'Planting Native Trees and Shrubs' by K.G. Beckett 1993, available from BSBI, Green Acre, Wood Lane, Peterborough PE8 5TP at £9.00 (incl. p&p).

BRITISH ASSOCIATION OF LANDSCAPE INDUSTRIES
Landscape House, Henry Street, Keighley, West Yorkshire BD21 3DR
Tel 01535 606139
Formed in 1972, BALI's principal objective is to encourage high standards of landscape contracting. Members' services cover the full spectrum of landscaping, both interior and exterior, design, construction and maintenance.

CENTRE FOR THE CONSERVATION OF HISTORIC PARKS AND GARDENS
Institute of Advanced Architectural Studies, University of York, The King's Manor, York YO1 2EP
Tel 01904 433988

COUNTRYSIDE COMMISSION
John Dower House, Crescent Place, Cheltenham GL50 3RA
Tel 01242 521381

COUNTRYSIDE COUNCIL FOR WALES
Plas Penrhos, Ffordd, Bangor, Gwynedd LL57 2LQ
Tel 01248 370444
Formed in 1992 by the merger of the Countryside Commission and the nature Conservancy Council within Wales.

ENGLISH NATURE
Northminster House, Peterborough PE1 1UA
Tel 01733340345

ENGLISH TOURIST BOARD
Thames Tower, Black's Road, London W6 9EL
Tel 0181 846 9000

THE FOUNTAIN SOCIETY
16 Gayfere Street, Smith Square, London SW1
Tel 0171 222 2917

FORESTRY COMMISSION
231 Corstophine Road, Edinburgh EH12 7AT
Tel 0131334 0303
Information, advice and grant aid under the Woodland Grant Scheme for the planting and management of woodlands.

THE GARDEN HISTORY SOCIETY
Station House, Church Lane, Wickwar, Glos. GL12 8NB
Tel 01454 294888
The GHS is the foremost national society for the study and protection of historic parks and gardens, providing advice on their conservation to owners and planning authorities, as well as a programme of educational activities and publications to members.

HORTICULTURAL TRADES ASSOCIATION
19 High Street, Theale, Reading RG7 5AH
Tel 01734 303132

INSTITUTE OF HORTICULTURE
PO Box 313, 80 Vincent Square, London SW1P 2PE
Tel 0171 976 5951

INSTITUTE OF LEISURE AND AMENITY MANAGEMENT
ILAM House, Lower Basildon, Reading, Berkshire RG8 9NE
Tel 01491 874222

JOINT COUNCIL FOR LANDSCAPE INDUSTRIES
c/o Horticultural Trades Association, 19 High Street, Theale, Reading RG7 5AH

LANDSCAPE DESIGN TRUST
13a West Street, Reigate, Surrey RH2 9BL
Tel 01737 223144
Publishers of "Researching a Garden's History" by David Lambert, Centre for the Conservation of Historic Parks & Gardens, available by mail order, price £5.20 inc. p&p.

THE LANDSCAPE INSTITUTE
6/7 Barnard Mews, London SW11
Tel 0171 738 9166

MUSEUM OF GARDEN HISTORY
5 Lambeth Palace Road, London SE1 7LB
Tel 0171 261 1891
The Museum, a charitable trust, was founded to commemorate the two John Tradescants, Royal Gardeners to Charles I & II, plant-hunters and collectors of rareties. Its aim is to display the history of gardens and to provide facilities for study. A replica 17th Century garden has been created. Books are available in the book shop.

NATIONAL STATELY HOME HOTLINE
c/o Ripley Castle, Ripley, Nr Harrogate, North Yorkshire HG3 3AY
Tel 01423 770152

NATIONAL COUNCIL FOR THE CONSERVATION OF PLANTS AND GARDENS
The Pines, Wisley Gardens, Woking, Surrey GU23 6QB
Tel 01483 211465
Conservation of our garden plant heritage through a network of nearly 600 national plant collections covering over 400 different genera, conserving many thousands of historic plants, many of which are no longer available commercially. Main publications: National Plant Collections Directory and the Pink Sheet (listing 1,500 uncommon plants).

NATIONAL TURFGRASS COUNCIL
Hunters Lodge, Dr Brown's Road, Minchinhampton, Stroud GL6 9BT
Tel 01453 883588

PROFESSIONAL GARDENERS GUILD
Head Gardener's House, Harewood House, Harewood, Leeds LS17 9LF
Tel 01532 886227
A national society for Head and single-handed gardeners employed in private gardens or in those run in a similar way, large or small. The Guild encourages communication between gardeners, publishes a quarterly newsletter and arranges meetings and garden visits.

PROFESSIONAL PLANT USERS GROUP
c/o The Landscape Institute, 6-7 Barnard Mews, London SW11 1QU
Tel 0171 738 9166

ROYAL BOTANIC GARDENS
Kew, Richmond, Surrey TW9 3AB
Tel 0181 940 1171

ROYAL FORESTRY SOCIETY OF ENGLAND WALES & NORTHERN IRELAND
102 High Street, Tring, Herts HP23 4AF
Tel 01442 822028
For over a century the RFS has spread knowledge about trees, woodlands and forests, and encouraged the multi-purpose, sustainable management of this vital renewable natural resource.

ROYAL HORTICULTURAL SOCIETY
80 Vincent Square, London SW1P 2PE
Tel 0171 834 4333
The Society provides inspiration to gardeners through it's shows and gardens and has an extensive programme of education, conservation and scientific research to ensure future generations can enjoy our gardening heritage too. A free advisory service, the monthly magazine The Garden and other benefits are provided to members.

SCOTTISH NATURAL HERITAGE
12 Hope Terrace, Edinburgh EH9 2AS
Tel 0131 332 2433
Formed in 1992 by the merger of the Countryside Commission for Scotland and the Nature Conservancy Council within Scotland.

SCOTTISH TOURIST BOARD
23 Ravelston Terrace, Edinburgh EH9 2AS
Tel 0131 332 2433

SOCIETY OF GARDEN DESIGNERS
6 Borough Road, Kingston upon Thames, Surrey KT2 6BD
Tel 0181 974 9483
The Society encourages a wide range of professional designers, many of whom specialise in, or have worked within the framework of, historic gardens. The Society publishes a quarterly journal concentrating on garden design issues.

THE TREE COUNCIL
35 Belgrave Square, London SW1X 8QN
Tel 0171 235 8854
The Council promotes the planting of trees, disseminates knowledge about trees and their management, acts as a forum for national problem identification and provides initiatives for co-operation. National Tree Week, the Tree Warden Scheme, publications, forums and conferences are sponsored. The Council also runs it own tree planting grant scheme.

WALES TOURIST BOARD
Brunnel House, 2 Fitzalan Road, Cardiff CF2 1UY
Tel 01222 499909

THE WOODLAND TRUST
Autumn Park, Dysart Road, Grantham, Lincolnshire NG31 6LL
Tel 01476 74297

OTHER ORGANISATIONS

ANCIENT MONUMENTS SOCIETY
St Ann's Vestry Hall, 2 Church Entry,
London EC4V 5HB
Tel 0171 236 3934

**ARCHITECTURAL AND HERITAGE
SOCIETY OF SCOTLAND**
The Glasite Meeting House, 33 Barony Street,
Edinburgh EH3 6NY
Tel 0131 557 0019

ART AND ANTIQUES SQUAD
New Scotland Yard, Broadway
London SW1H 0BG
Tel 0171 230 1212

**ASSOCIATION OF CONSERVATION
OFFICERS**
24 Middle Street, Stroud GL5 1DZ
Tel 01453 753949

**ASSOCIATION OF CONSERVATION
OFFICERS (SCOTLAND)**
The Glasite Meeting House,
33 Barony Street, Edinburgh EH3 6NX
Tel 0131 529 3913

**CADW (WELSH HISTORIC
MONUMENTS)**
Brunel House, 2 Fitzalan Road,
Cardiff CF2 1UY
Tel 01222 465511

THE CIVIC TRUST
17 Carlton House Terrace, London
SW1Y 5AW
Tel 0171 930 0914

THE CIVIC TRUST FOR WALES
4th Floor, Empire House,
Mount Stewart Square,
Cardiff CF1 6DN
Tel 01222 484606

**COUNCIL FOR BRITISH
ARCHAEOLOGY**
Bowes Morrel House, 111 Walmgate,
York YO1 2UA
Tel 01904 671417

**COUNCIL FOR SCOTTISH
ARCHAEOLOGY**
c/o National Museums of Scotland,
Queen Street, Edinburgh EH2 1JD
Tel 0131 225 7534

ENGLISH HERITAGE
Fortress House, 23 Savile Row,
London W1X 1AB
Tel 0171 973 3000

THE GEORGIAN GROUP
37 Spital Square, London E1 6DY
Tel 0171 377 1722

HISTORIC HOUSES ASSOCIATION
2 Chester Street, London SW1X 7BB
Tel 0171 259 5688

HISTORIC SCOTLAND
20 Brandon Street, Edinburgh EH3 5RA
Tel 0131 244 3144

**INSTITUTE OF FIELD
ARCHAEOLOGISTS**
Metallurgy & Materials Building,
University of Birmingham,
Edgbaston, Birmingham B15 2TT
Tel 0121 471 2788

**INTERNATIONAL COUNCIL ON
MONUMENTS & SITES UK**
10 Barley Mow Passage, Chiswick,
London W4 4PH
Tel 0181 994 6477
Through its Historic Gardens and Landscapes
Committee, ICOMOS UK promotes policy
development and good practice in garden and
landscape conservation. Publications include
seminar papers.

**NATIONAL HERITAGE MEMORIAL
FUND**
10 St James's Street, London SW1A 1EF
Tel 0171 930 0963

THE NATIONAL TRUST
36 Queen Anne's Gate, London SW1H 9AS
Tel 0171 222 9251

**THE NATIONAL TRUST FOR
SCOTLAND**
5 Charlotte Square, Edinburgh EH2 4DU
Tel 0131 226 5922

**ROYAL COMMISSION ON THE
ANCIENT AND HISTORICAL
MONUMENTS OF SCOTLAND**
John Sinclair House, 16 Bernard Terrace,
Edinburgh EH8 9NX
Tel 0131 662 1456
National Monuments Record of Scotland
holds documentary photography, drawn and
mapped records of all kinds of historic
landscape types.

**ROYAL COMMISSION ON THE
ANCIENT AND HISTORICAL
MONUMENTS OF WALES**
Crown Buildings, Plas Crug, Aberystwyth,
Dyfed SY23 1NJ
Tel 01970 624381

**ROYAL COMMISSION ON THE
HISTORICAL MONUMENTS OF
ENGLAND**
National Monuments Record Centre,
Kemble Drive, Swindon SN2 2GZ
Tel 01793 414700

**ROYAL INCORPORATION OF
ARCHITECTS IN SCOTLAND**
15 Rutland Square, Edinburgh
Tel 0131 229 7239

**ROYAL INSTITUTE OF BRITISH
ARCHITECTS**
66 Portland Place, London W1N 4AD
Tel 0171 580 5533

**ROYAL INSTITUTION OF CHARTERED
SURVEYORS**
12 Great George Street, Parliament Square,
London SW1P 3AD
Tel 0171 222 7000

SAVE BRITAIN'S HERITAGE
68 Battersea High Street, London SW11 3HX
Tel 0171 228 3336

THE SCOTTISH CIVIC TRUST
24 George Square, Glasgow G2 1EF
Tel 0141 221 1466

SCOTTISH CONSERVATION BUREAU
3 Stenhouse Mill Lane, Edinburgh
EH11 3LR
Tel 0131 443 1666

**THE SCOTTISH SOCIETY FOR
CONSERVATION AND RESTORATION**
The Glasite Meeting House,
33 Barony Street, Edinburgh EH1 6NX
Tel 0131 557 0049

**THE SOCIETY FOR THE PROTECTION
OF ANCIENT BUILDINGS**
37 Spital Square, London E1 6DY
Tel 0171 377 1644

THE TEMPLE TRUST
c/o Gunnersbury Park Museum, Popes
Lane, London W3 8LQ
Tel 0181 992 2248
Founded in 1994, the Temple Trust aims to
raise funds to restore and preserve historic
ornamental landscape 'follies' and Neo
Classical and Palladian buildings, initially
targeting those in public open spaces.
Currently running fund-raising exhibitions
and concerts in the Temple, Gunnersbury
Park, London W3.

TWENTIETH CENTURY SOCIETY
Environmental Institute, Bolton Road
Swinton M27 2UX
Tel 0161 793 9898

THE VICTORIAN SOCIETY
1 Priory Gardens, Bedford Park, London
W4 1TT
Tel 0181 994 1019
The report Public Prospects, Historic Urban
Parks Under Threat, jointly published with the
Garden History Society, is available from the
Society, £5.00.

ARCHAEOLOGISTS

LANCASTER UNIVERSITY ARCHAEOLOGICAL UNIT
See advertisement on page 8.

ARCHITECTS AND LANDSCAPE ARCHITECTS

BROADWAY MALYAN CONSERVATION
See article on page 25.

THE LANDSCAPE
• *p r a c t i c e* •

Ainderby Hall

Ainderby Steeple
Northallerton
North Yorkshire DL7 9QJ

Tel: 01609 77 2554 Fax: 01609 77 3322

NICHOLAS PEARSON ASSOCIATES LTD

Creech Grange, Dorset

30 Brock Street, Bath BA1 2LN
Tel 01225 445548
Fax 01225 312387
Our experienced team has worked on more than forty historic sites across Britain, helping owners with grant aid and a range of restoration and management projects, including parkland, lakes, gardens, and historic woodlands. Our freshness of vision has led to sensitive design solutions and new ideas for income generation.

STUART PAGE ARCHITECTS
See advertisement on page 24.

COURSES

THE ARCHITECTURAL ASSOCIATION
See advertisement on page 8.

CAPEL MANOR HORTICULTURAL & ENVIRONMENTAL CENTRE

Bullsmoor Lane, Enfield,
Middlesex EN1 4RQ
Tel 0181 366 4442
Fax 01992 717544
Greater London's only specialist college of Horticulture and Countryside studies with gardens open. Full and part-time courses, including the exclusive BTEC National Diploma in Heritage Gardens, organised in conjunction with the Historic Houses Association and Professional Gardeners Guild. (Sponsorship opportunities available).

MOULTON COLLEGE
See advertisement on page 8.

THE UNIVERSITY OF YORK, INSTITUTE OF ADVANCED ARCHITECTURAL STUDIES
See advertisement on page 8.

FLOWER POTS & URNS

CAPITAL GARDEN PRODUCTS LTD

Gibbs Reed Barn,
Pashley Road, Ticehurst,
East Sussex TN5 7HE
Tel 01580 201092
Fax 01580 201093
Urns, water cisterns, troughs in cast lead, Faux-lead, Bronzage. Commissions and reproductions with coats-of-arms and dates our speciality.

WHICHFORD POTTERY
See advertisement on page 16.

GARDEN BUILDINGS

COWIE & ROBERTS
See advertisement on page 10.

GALES OF MORETONHAMPSTEAD

Court Street,
Moretonhampstead,
Devon TQ13 8LH
Tel 01647 440607
Fax 01647 440132
Manufacturers of high quality sheds, workshops, stables and stores using 'Tanalised' British grown softwoods. Suppliers of fencing materials and manufacturers of farm buildings.

THE MORTON PARTNERSHIP LTD
Structural and Civil Engineers

61 Islington Park Street,
London N1 1QB
Tel 0171 359 0202
Fax 0171 354 2925
and
3a London Road, Halesworth,
Suffolk IP19 8LH
Tel 01986 875 651
Fax 01986 875 085
Brian Morton founded this practice in 1966. It is now completely involved in minimum repair solutions to preserve historic buildings. Services include preliminary advice, structural surveys and presentation of the most cost effective solution to the proper repair of historic buildings. In addition to the many projects undertaken with buildings of national importance, work to small buildings is an important part of their work.

RAFFLES THATCHED GARDEN BUILDINGS
See advertisement on the inside front cover.

TOWN & COUNTRY CONSERVATORIES

Fine Glass Buildings Ltd,
Horningtoft, Dereham,
Norfolk NR20 5DY
Tel 01328 700565
Fax 01328 700015,
or
London office:
Unit 48, Eurolink,
49 Effra Road,
London SW2 1BZ
Tel 0171 924 9270
Fax 0171 737 4334
The company's London design office has considerable experience of working closely with professional bodies, and boasts an impressive portfolio of projects on listed buildings and in conservation areas.
The Norfolk joinery workshops build these conservatories, summer houses, orangeries and roof lights in wholly traditional materials, incorporating modern technology with period style.

Please also refer to advertisement on page 10.

WEST COUNTRY BUILDINGS

Moreton Works,
Clovelly Road,
Bideford,
Devon EX39 3QU
Tel/Fax 01237 472227
Manufacturers of traditional strong timber buildings designed to last, with a range from garden sheds to summer houses. Also manufacturers of quality timber fencing panels and gates. We offer tailor made solutions for your storage problems, fencing and leisure building requirements. Suppliers to councils, garden centres, builders and farmers merchants.

GARDEN FURNITURE

JULIAN CHICHESTER DESIGNS

33 Parsons Green Lane,
London SW6 4HH
Tel 0171 371 9055
Fax 0171 371 9066
Julian Chichester Designs offers a collection of fine English 18th & 19th Century style garden furniture. The furniture combines strength with fine and graceful lines making it a beautiful feature in any setting.

THE TEAK TIGER TRADING COMPANY

Sudbury, Suffolk CO10 8YZ
Tel 01787 880900
Fax 01787 880906
Suppliers of quality, solid (plantation grown) teak outdoor furniture. A range of benches, chairs and tables ideal for park or garden use. The furniture can be left outside all year round without requiring any maintenance.

HORTICULTURAL CONSULTANTS

PHILIP SWINDELLS ASSOCIATES
See advertisement on page 26.

IRRIGATION SERVICES

H₂O IRRIGATION LTD
See advertisement on page 22.

LANDSCAPING SERVICES – NATURAL SOUND BARRIERS

C D BROWN (LANDSCAPING) LTD
See advertisement on page 24.

METALWORK – GATES & RAILINGS

ANWICK FORGE
See advertisement on page 26.

D. C. & S. BROADBENT ENGINEERING
See advertisement on page 26.

GATE-A-MATION
See advertisement on page 30.

RUPERT HARRIS METALWORK AND SCULPTURE RESTORATION
See advertisement on page 10.

NURSERIES

KELWAYS LIMITED
See advertisement on page 16.

PETER BEALES ROSES HGL
London Road, Attleborough,
Norfolk NR17 1AY
Tel 01953 454707
The largest collection of genuine old roses. Embracing shrubs, climbers, ramblers and the most garden-worthy varieties of recent times, of which over 200 classics are unique to us. A comprehensive, full colour catalogue is available on request.

PAVING

TOWN & COUNTRY GARDENS
See advertisement on page 24.

PUBLICATIONS

ROYAL HORTICULTURAL SOCIETY DICTIONARY OF GARDENING
The MacMillan Press Limited
See advertisement on page 16.

PERSPECTIVES ON ARCHITECTURE
See advertisement on page 10.

RECONSTRUCTED STONE PRODUCTS

CHILSTONE

Sprivers, Horsmonden,
Kent TN12 8DR
Tel 01892 723 266
Fax 01892 723223
Chilstone is a quality reconstituted stone, handmade to a very high standard. Natural Chilstone is buff-coloured, between Portland and Bath stone in colour. Chilstone has been used in numerous historic gardens –Warwick and Hever Castles, Kew, Regents Park and Buckingham Palace. We work with the DoE, National Trust and English Heritage.

HADDONSTONE LIMITED
See advertisement on page 24.

SECURITY

CLARKE INSTRUMENTS LTD
2 Dolphin Industrial Estate,
Southampton Road, Salisbury,
Wiltshire SP1 1NB
Tel 01179 323 451
Electro-mechanical access control/ security equipment.

FOCAS LTD
Unit 4c, Cheney Manor
Industrial Estate, Swindon,
Wiltshire SN2 2PJ
Tel 01793 513200
Statue alarms.

GATE-A-MATION AUTOMATIC GATE SYSTEMS
See advertisement on page 30.

MITSUI MACHINERY SALES (UK) LTD
Sopwith Drive, Brooklands,
Weybridge, Surrey KT13 0UZ
Tel 01932 358000
Datatag systems and transponders.

VSPS SECURITY PRODUCTS
20 Coniston Road, Blackrod,
Bolton, Lancashire BL6 5DN
Tel 01204 691745
Telescopic anti-ram raid bollards.

STATUARY CONSERVATION

CLIVEDEN CONSERVATION WORKSHOPS LTD
See advertisement on page 16.

TURF

NICKERSONS TURF FARMS
See article on page 29.

Planning Requirements

The Orangery, Kensington Palace, London

WHAT ALTERATIONS REQUIRE CONSENT?

Alterations to parks and gardens generally do not require statutory consent unless they affect planning requirements designed to protect buildings and some trees. In England the effect of proposals on a park or garden or its setting which is included in English Heritage's Register of Historic Parks and Gardens of Special Historic Interest is a material consideration in the determination of a planning application, and local planning authorities should now protect registered parks and gardens in preparing development plans and in determining planning applications. (C.f. David Lambert's article on page 2).

In Scotland the position is broadly similar: planning authorities are encouraged through the Scottish Office Planning Advice Notes series and other published guidance to adopt policies in their development plans to protect historic gardens and designed landscapes. Also, planning authorities are required to consult Historic Scotland and Scottish Natural Heritage on planning applications which affect a garden or designed landscape included in the Inventory of Gardens and Designed Landscapes in Scotland (published in 1988). Planning authorities may be required by a Direction to notify decisions on such applications to the Secretary of State for Scotland before planning permission is granted.

In England and Wales planning is governed by the *Town & Country Planning Act 1990* and the *Planning (Listed Buildings and Conservation Areas) Act 1990*, while in Scotland it is governed by the *Town & Country Planning (Scotland) Act 1972*. The consents which are required are essentially the same, and application for consent should always be made to the local planning authority for the following:

PLANNING PERMISSION

The development of a new building and most external alterations and extensions to an existing building require planning permission. However certain small extensions and other alterations can be made to a house without planning permission, under *Permitted Development Rights* which are detailed in the *General Development Order*. (*PD Rights* do not apply to flats).

LISTED BUILDING CONSENT

This consent is required for the alterations and demolitions of listed buildings and their interiors, as well as of any objects or structures which lie within the curtilage and which were constructed before 1 July 1948. This may be taken to include garden walls, sundials, dovecotes and other such objects and structures as well as buildings which are ancillary to the principal building, not separated from it, and were so at the time of listing. It is important to note that alterations to a listed building without consent is a criminal offence, and is therefore imprisonable.

CONSERVATION AREA CONSENT

The demolition of a building or of any part of a building which lies within a conservation area requires consent. This includes the demolition of key features of a building which may be considered to affect the character or appearance of the conservation area.

Dovecote and fountain, Holland Park, London

WORKS TO TREES SUBJECT TO A TREE PRESERVATION ORDER

The consent of the local planning authority is required to cut down, top, or lop a tree which is protected by a *Tree Preservation Order (TPO)*. The principal exception to this is where a tree is dying, dead or dangerous. In which case at least five day's notice should be given to the local authority, except in an emergency.

NOTIFICATION OF PROPOSED WORKS TO TREES IN CONSERVATION AREAS

Within a conservation area anyone proposing to cut down, top or lop a tree in a conservation area is required to give the local planning authority six weeks notice.

NOTE

For further information on listed building and conservation areas consult the Building Conservation Directory.